SOCIAL ISSUES, JUSTICE AND STATUS

SOCIAL ISOLATION, PARTICIPATION AND IMPACT ON MENTAL HEALTH

KRISTIN T. ROWE
EDITOR

nova publishers
New York

Library of Congress Cataloging-in-Publication Data

Social isolation, participation and impact on mental health / editor, Kristin T. Rowe.
pages cm. -- (Social issues, justice and status)
Includes index.
ISBN 978-1-63482-505-4 (hardcover)
1. Social isolation. 2. Social participation. 3. Mental health. I. Rowe, Kristin T.
HM1131.S655 2015
302.5'45--dc23
2015009608

Published by Nova Science Publishers, Inc. † New York

CONTENTS

PREFACE

Classic and contemporary theories, based on evolutionary, social, and developmental perspectives, argue that humans are motivated from the very earliest days of life to seek, establish and maintain social interactions and close relationships with others. For any species with a social nature, isolation from other con-specific members is an environmental deprivation of a basic need. This book examines participation in society and the impact social isolation has on mental health.

Chapter 1 – Rationale: As older adults represent a large and growing part of our society, it is crucial to improve their health and well-being. Recognized as a determinant of health, social participation is influenced by the community. Indeed, a high level of participation in community activities (cultural, religious, physical, neighborhood, volunteering, etc.) can be achieved in a favorable environment (universal accessibility, availability of transportation, social participation opportunities, safety and social support). A better understanding of the distribution of social participation according to population demography and geography, such as gender and age, location, and reasons for not participating, is required for the creation of favorable environments. However, little is known about this distribution and the differences between populations. Objective: This chapter aimed to describe and compare social participation among older Canadians according to gender, age (45-64 vs. 65+), transportation and location (province/region and metropolitan vs non-metropolitan area). Respondents' desire to participate more and reasons for restrictions in participation were also explored. Method: Secondary analysis of aggregated data from the cross-sectional 2008-2009 Canadian Community Health Survey, including the "Healthy Aging" thematic was done. The survey involved 30,865 Canadians aged 45 and over, and collected information related to health, lifestyle, social and economic issues. Social participation was measured by the frequency of involvement in eight community activities per month. Chi-square tests followed by pairwise comparisons were performed to identify differences according to gender, age and location. Geographic visualisation complemented statistical analysis. Results: Canadians participated in an average of 12.8 activities per month, and women tended to be slightly more involved than men (13.1 vs. 12.5). For both genders, the three most important activities were family or friends, religious and physical activities. On average older Canadians participated more in religious activities (2.4 vs. 1.6), while younger ones tended to participate more in physical (2.4 vs. 1.7) and educational (1.4 vs. 0.9) activities. Canadians aged 65 and over with a driver's license participated more than those aged 45-64 (13.3 vs. 9.4). Quebecers participated least, while residents of the Prairies were the most involved in community activities (11.9 and 13.8). More Canadians aged 45-64 wanted to participate more in community activities than those aged 65 and over (36.8% vs. 23.9%), and women more than men (34.3% vs. 30.9%). However, environmental barriers, such as respondents not wanting to go alone, cost and transportation problems, restricted women more than men in both age groups. For women aged 65 and over, location inaccessibility (1.7% vs. 0.7%) and the unavailability of activities (8.0% vs. 5.4%) restricted their participation. The unavailability of activities was a barrier for 10% of women in the Atlantic region and Prairies, and also restricted older Canadians who lived in non-census metropolitan areas (non-CMAs) more than in CMAs (8.0% vs. 4.8%). Conclusion: This chapter suggests that demography and geography are important factors to consider to better understand older Canadians' social participation. Compared to men, women reported more environmental barriers, especially if aged 65 and over. Some barriers, such as unavailability and inaccessibility, were mostly reported in the Atlantic region and Prairies. Further research examining respondents' locations in greater detail is needed to foster the creation of an environment that improves social participation of older Canadians.

Chapter 2 – The present of potential social isolation factors on the psychological outcomes of immigrant youth in early adolescent. Data are derived from the New Canadian Children and Youth Study (NCCYS), a national longitudinal survey including 459 immigrant youth aged 11 to13 years living in the Greater Montreal region, Canada from five ethnic groups (Mainland China, Hong Kong, the Philippines, Haiti, and Lebanon). Four social isolation factors in relation to peers are included as predictors: perceived peer rejection based on ethnic background, feelings of disconnectedness from

SOCIAL ISSUES, JUSTICE AND STATUS

SOCIAL ISOLATION, PARTICIPATION AND IMPACT ON MENTAL HEALTH

SOCIAL ISSUES, JUSTICE AND STATUS

Additional books in this series can be found on Nova's website under the Series tab.

Additional e-books in this series can be found on Nova's website under the e-book tab.

others, perceived relationships with peers, and the absence of close friendships. Self-esteem and emotional distress are included as psychological outcomes. Multivariate analyses are performed to examine the effects of the social isolation factors on self-esteem and emotional distress of immigrant youth. The results show that peer rejection based on ethnic background, feelings of disconnectedness, and perceived relationships with peers are significantly associated with self-esteem and emotional distress, after controlling for demographic background variables. Significant variations across ethnic groups are also found in feelings of disconnectedness from others, the absence of close friendships, perceived relationships with peers, and emotional distress. These findings suggest that social isolation experiences in relation to peer interactions are critical factors affecting self-esteem and emotional distress of early adolescent immigrants. The findings and implications are discussed with respect to the social contexts of the lives of immigrant youth and migration-related issues.

Chapter 3 – The aim of the present study was to identify which aspects relating to appearance-related concerns and social experiences, and status amongst peers, are relevant to understanding social isolation in early adolescents. In a sample 387 boys and girls (M_{age} = 12.0 years, 44.4% males), the authors assessed both objective and subjective indicators of social isolation. Specifically, social isolation was measured based on adolescents' self-reported loneliness, inhibition in social contexts, and social acceptance. They also used nominations of friendship to identify youth who had no reciprocated friends (total friendlessness) or whose closest friend was not reciprocated (close friendlessness). As predicted, adolescents who felt socially isolated (i.e., inhibited, lonely, or low social acceptance), reported more dissatisfaction with their body and concerns about peer rejection because of the way they look, as well as elevated appearance teasing by peers and by family members. These youth were also less accepted by their peers. Notably, adolescents who felt inhibited, lonely, or less socially accepted were not more likely to be friendless. Finally, adolescents were at increased odds of both total and close friendlessness when they were less accepted by their peers, while the odds of close friendlessness were higher among adolescents who reported higher body dissatisfaction and, surprisingly, lower among those who reported more appearance teasing from family members. The results of this study have implications for supporting socially isolated and vulnerable youth, and highlight the need for continued research to examine the longitudinal associations of social isolation with appearance-related concerns and social adversity.

Chapter 4 – For any species with a social nature, isolation from other conspecific members is an environmental deprivation of a basic need. The sequelae of social isolation are multifarious, and may relate clinically to physiological and psychological abnormalities. The epigenetic theory holds that an unsatisfactory resolution of a particular stage would reflect a failure afterwards, thus raises the existence of a hypothetically critical time window during early life in which a temporary isolation rearing (IR) after weanling determines principally for physical, cognitive or emotional performance in adulthood. However, evidence also revealed that a long term, ongoing and cumulative IR since the weanling caused different, and sometime opposite effects in neural substrates and networks. It is therefore that the timing and the length of time play different roles in the IR effects, as they represent distinctive neural mechanisms for the individual to copy with the deprivation of social need. Based on the current developmental theories, the present article reviews the related IR works to date with an attempt to interpret the effects of social isolation in terms of social need, behavioral inhibition, cumulative stress and mismatch hypothesis, dopaminergic activity, and particularly addresses the importance of both the timing and the persistence of social isolation.

In: Social Isolation, Participation …
Editor: Kristin T. Rowe

ISBN: 978-1-63482-505-4

Chapter 1

Social Participation and Environmental Barriers among Aging Canadians: Distribution and Differences in Gender, Age and Location

Daniel Naud and Mélanie Levasseur
Research Center on Aging, Faculty of Medicine and Health Sciences, University of Sherbrooke, Canada

Abstract

Rationale: As older adults represent a large and growing part of our society, it is crucial to improve their health and well-being. Recognized as a determinant of health, social participation is influenced by the community. Indeed, a high level of participation in community activities (cultural, religious, physical, neighborhood, volunteering, etc.) can be achieved in a favorable environment (universal accessibility, availability of transportation, social participation opportunities, safety and social support). A better understanding of the distribution of social participation according to population demography and geography, such as gender and age, location, and reasons for not participating, is required for the creation of favorable environments. However, little is known about this distribution and the differences between populations.

Objective: This chapter aimed to describe and compare social participation among older Canadians according to gender, age (45-64 vs. 65+), transportation and location (province/region and metropolitan vs non-metropolitan area). Respondents' desire to participate more and reasons for restrictions in participation were also explored.

Method: Secondary analysis of aggregated data from the cross-sectional 2008-2009 Canadian Community Health Survey, including the "Healthy Aging" thematic was done. The survey involved 30,865 Canadians aged 45 and over, and collected information related to health, lifestyle, social and economic issues. Social participation was measured by the frequency of involvement in eight community activities per month. Chi-square tests followed by pairwise comparisons were performed to identify differences according to gender, age and location. Geographic visualisation complemented statistical analysis.

Results: Canadians participated in an average of 12.8 activities per month, and women tended to be slightly more involved than men (13.1 vs. 12.5). For both genders, the three most important activities were family or friends, religious and physical activities. On average older Canadians participated more in religious activities (2.4 vs. 1.6), while younger ones tended to participate more in physical (2.4 vs. 1.7) and educational (1.4 vs. 0.9) activities. Canadians aged 65 and over with a driver's license participated more than those aged 45-64 (13.3 vs. 9.4). Quebecers participated least, while residents of the Prairies were the most involved in community activities (11.9 and 13.8). More Canadians aged 45-64 wanted to participate more in community activities than those aged 65 and over (36.8% vs. 23.9%), and women more than men (34.3% vs. 30.9%). However, environmental barriers, such as respondents not wanting to go alone, cost and transportation problems, restricted women more than men in both age groups. For women aged 65 and over, location inaccessibility (1.7% vs. 0.7%) and the unavailability of activities (8.0% vs. 5.4%) restricted their participation. The unavailability of activities was a barrier for 10% of women in the Atlantic region and Prairies, and also restricted older Canadians who lived in non-census metropolitan areas (non-CMAs) more than in CMAs (8.0% vs. 4.8%).

Conclusion: This chapter suggests that demography and geography are important factors to consider to better understand older Canadians' social participation. Compared to men, women reported more environmental barriers, especially if aged 65 and over. Some barriers, such as unavailability and inaccessibility, were mostly reported in the Atlantic region and Prairies. Further research examining respondents' locations in greater detail is needed to foster the creation of an environment that improves social participation of older Canadians.

INTRODUCTION

The reshaping of the world's demography impels us to develop a better understanding of community environments and their health implications. Due to increased longevity, declining fertility and the aging of baby boom generations (United Nations, 2000), older adults represent a growing share of the population. Although Canada is among a younger group of developed countries, its population aged 65 and over was estimated to be 15.7% in 2014 (Lebel & Charbonneau, 2014). This proportion is predicted to reach between 24.3% and 27.6% by 2046 (McDaniel & Rozanova, 2011). As we age, health and functional independence decline, secondary to chronic conditions such as arthritis and heart or back problems. Indeed, the majority (76%) of Canadians aged 65 and over reported at least one chronic condition (Canadian Institute for Health Information, 2011).

Defined as a person's involvement in community activities that provide social interactions within the community or society (Levasseur, Richard, Gauvin & Raymond, 2010), social participation is a determinant of well-being for older adults (Adams, Leibbrandt & Moon, 2011). Moreover, social participation is positively associated with decreased mortality (Seeman, 2000; Walsh et al., 2013; Wilkins, 2003), disability (de Leon, Glass & Berkman, 2003; Levasseur et al., 2010; Lund, Nilsson & Avlund, 2010), depression (Fiori, Antonucci & Cortina, 2006; Glass, De Leon, Bassuk & Berkman, 2006; Li & Ferraro, 2005) and cognitive decline (Engelhardt, Buber, Skirbekk & Prskawetz, 2010).

Recognized as a determinant of health and according to the World Health Organization's Commission on Social Determinants of Health (Marmot, Friel, Bell, Houweling & Taylor, 2008), social participation is influenced by the neighborhood physical and social environment. The neighborhood environment may affect social participation in two broad ways: First, as an environmental buoyancy, facilitating access to resources and social support (Glass & Balfour, 2003), second, as an environmental pressure, challenging personal competencies through obstacles to mobility, attitudes and physical barriers (Lawton, 1986). The neighborhood environment can be defined, on the one hand, by physical features such as urban design, traffic density and speed, distance to and design of resources for physical activities, esthetics, crime and safety (Davison & Lawson, 2006). Although where one lives can impact resource availability and transportation, studies have shown that older adults' social participation is similar in rural and urban areas (Levasseur et al., In Press; Therrien & Desrosiers, 2010). Nevertheless, barriers to participation can differ. For example, transportation can influence intra-regional mobility, with studies showing that a driver's license is positively associated with social participation (Levasseur et al., In Press) and driving is the preferred mode of transportation among older adults (Cao, Mokhtarian & Handy, 2010). On the other hand, social aspects of the environment are also important factors influencing social participation: support and association, attitudes, services, infrastructures and policies (Webber, Porter & Menec, 2010).

Because strategies addressing social issues such as isolation are very cost-effective (Heyden, 1998; Valtorta & Hanratty, 2012), it is essential for public health actors to consider interventions aimed at improving social participation in their community. A better understanding of social participation distribution and differences according to population characteristics such as gender and age, location, and reasons for not participating, is required for the creation of favorable environments. However, little is known about this distribution or the differences. This chapter thus aimed to describe and compare social participation among older Canadians according to gender, age (45-64 vs 65+), transportation and location (province/region and metropolitan vs non-metropolitan areas). Respondents' desire to participate more and barriers to community activities were also explored.

METHOD

Secondary analysis of aggregated data from the cross-sectional 2008-2009 Canadian Community Health Survey (CCHS) including the "Healthy Aging" thematic was done, using publically available data from Statistics Canada (2008-2009). The survey, on site and computer-assisted, was conducted among Canadians aged 45 and over living in private dwellings (thus excluding people living in collective dwellings and institutions) in ten provinces. A stratified random sampling strategy was used to recruit respondents based on age, gender, province, and rural or urban area. Information related to health, lifestyle and socioeconomic characteristics was collected. Full-time members of the Canadian Forces and residents of the three territories, Indian reserves, Crown lands and some remote regions were excluded from the sampling. Response rates were 80.8% (household level), 92.1% (person level) and 74.4% (combined) for a total sample of 30,865 respondents, representative of older Canadians.

Variables and Measures

Sociodemographic characteristics were measured by a series of questions on gender, age, marital status, driver's license, transportation, retirement, dwelling, household income, immigration and education (Table 1). To preserve anonymity, age answers were aggregated by Statistics Canada in two age groups: 45 to 64 years old, and 65 and over. As comparing some answers between all ten provinces led to a very small number of respondents in some provinces (e.g., Prince Edward Island), respondents were grouped based on a five-region model (Atlantic, Quebec, Ontario, Prairies and British Columbia). To explore comparisons of social participation of Canadians living in highly urbanized areas, a second geographic variable was retained: living in a Census Metropolitan Area (CMA) or not. A CMA is made up of several municipalities that surround an urban core, with a population of at least 100,000 inhabitants (Statistics Canada, 2010b). *Physical health condition* was measured by asking respondents about chronic conditions (at least one; aggregated data), pain and discomfort (from no pain (1) to pain preventing most activities (5)), and mobility (from walking around the neighborhood without difficulty(1) to being unable to walk alone, even with walking equipment (4)). *Social support* was considered using the three-item loneliness scale (how often respondents feel they lack companionship, left out or isolated from others; from not lonely (3) to very lonely (9)) (Hughes, Waite, Hawkley & Cacioppo, 2004), and aggregated values concerning tangible social support (how often someone can help if confined to bed, can take him/her to the doctor, can prepare meals or do daily chores; from the lowest (0) to the highest (32) social support).

Social participation was assessed by measuring how often respondents reported participating in eight different activities: *Family or friends* activities outside the household; church or *religious* activities; sports or *physical* activities; *educational* and cultural activities; service *club* or fraternal organization activities; neighborhood, community or professional *association* activities; *volunteer* or charity work; and *other recreational* activities (e.g., hobbies, bingo and other games). Based on previous studies (Levasseur et al., In Press; Richard, Gauvin, Gosselin & Laforest, 2009; Richard et al., 2012), responses were converted into frequency of engagement per month for each activity ("at least once a week" = 6; "at least once a month" = 2; "at least once a year" = 1; and "never" = 0). Also to preserve anonymity, aggregated data combined the "almost every day" and "at least once a week" responses and did not allow respondent participation to be detailed further. Sum of activities resulted in a total social participation score representing the number of community activities per month. Moreover, for easier utilization in clinical situations (Desrosiers, Noreau & Rochette, 2004), the total social participation score was divided into quartiles, with the lowest (less than 6 activities / month) and the highest (more than 18 activities / month) quartiles being the reference of interest.

Respondents were asked if they *wanted to participate* in more social, recreational or group activities and, if so, to select one or more barriers that prevented them from participating, from a list of 12 barriers: Too busy; Health condition limitation; Personal or family responsibilities; Time of activities not suitable; Do not want to go alone; Cost; Activities not available in the area; Transportation problems; Location too far; Afraid or concerns about safety; Language-related reasons; Location not physically accessible; and Other.

Analysis

Respondents were described by means and standard deviations or frequencies and percentages according to the type of variable (continuous or categorical, respectively). Pairwise comparisons (z and t-tests, for means and column proportions, respectively) were performed to identify significant differences according to gender, age and location. P-values were adjusted using the Bonferroni method when carrying out pairwise comparisons of Canadian regions. Because weighted data are representative of the entire aging Canadian population (13,635,506), the sum of weights was brought back to the sample's *n* (30,865) to avoid mismeasurement of p-values (alpha = 0.01), which does not impact the estimates. Based on the coefficients of variation provided by Statistics Canada (2010a), enough respondents were available in each subgroup. Geographic visualisation was used to examine social participation across the country, to complement statistical analysis. A unique values scheme was applied to both maps, the number of spatial units being low enough to allow it. All statistical analyses were carried out using SPSS version 17.0 (SPSS Inc., 2008) and cartography was executed using ArcGIS version 10.1 (ESRI, 2011). The Statistics Canada Executive Management Board, acting as the Research Ethics Board, approved the CCHS Healthy Aging component. The public use microdata files must meet stringent security and confidentiality standards required by the *Statistics Act* before they are released for public access. Variables most likely to lead to identification of an individual are deleted from the data file or are collapsed to broader categories.

Results

The majority of the Canadians surveyed were aged between 45 and 64 (68.0%) and over half were women (51.9%; data not shown). Most were married, although fewer among Canadians aged 65 and over, where married was replaced by widowed (Table 1). A vast majority of Canadians aged 45 and over had a driver's license; however, one third of women aged 65 and over did not. Hence, driving a car was the most common form of transportation for a majority of the population, followed by being a passenger in a motor vehicle (Table 1). Alternative forms (public transit, paratransit, walking or cycling) accounted for about 10% of the most common forms of transportation. About one third of Canadians aged 65 and over were retired, fewer women than men. A large majority of respondents owned their dwelling in both age groups. Household income dropped significantly across the two groups (Table 1). More women than men were in the lowest income brackets. Approximately one out of four persons aged 45 and over was an immigrant. Compared respectively to older respondents and women, the younger age group and men had higher levels of education. Most aged Canadians reported having at least one chronic condition, with the proportion reaching about nine out of ten among Canadians aged 65 and over. Pain and discomfort as well as mobility restrictions tended to prevent more women than men from doing activities, although they did not prevent most Canadians. In general, aging Canadians did not feel very lonely. Men had moderately greater social support than women, especially in the group aged 65 and over.

Similarly across regions, approximately three out of four older Canadians were married (Table 2). A majority of the population in every region had a driver's license, with the Prairies and British Columbia, where nine out of ten people had a license, sharing the highest proportions. While Quebecers were least likely to drive a motor vehicle as the most common form of transportation, British Columbians were most likely to drive. Most Canadians aged 45 and over were not retired, with Quebec and the Prairies having respectively the lowest (6.6%) and highest (11.1%) proportions of retired persons. A vast majority of Canadians owned their dwelling, but more than one quarter in Quebec were renters. Household incomes were significantly higher in Ontario, the Prairies and British Columbia. More than a third of older Canadians living in Ontario and British Columbia were immigrants, while the Atlantic region had only 3.7%. Atlantic Canadians, especially women, had the highest proportion reporting at least one chronic condition, and British Columbia had the lowest.

Table 1. Sociodemographic characteristics of the aging Canadian population by age group and gender (% and mean)

		45-64			65 and over			Total		
		F	M	Total	F	M	Total	F	M	Total
Marital status	Married/ Common-law	76.5*	80.7	78.6**	49.5*	80.2	63.4	67.4*	80.6	73.7
	Widowed	4.0*	1.2	2.6**	37.8*	10.4	25.4	15.4*	4.0	9.9
	Divorced/ Separated	12.4*	9.8	11.1**	8.4*	6.2	7.4	11.1*	8.8	10.0
	Single	7.1*	8.2	7.6**	4.3*	3.2	3.8	6.1	6.7	6.4
Driver's license	Yes	89.0*	95.5	92.2**	63.4*	88.8	74.9	80.3*	93.5	86.7
	No	11.0*	4.5	7.8**	36.6*	11.2	25.1	19.7*	6.5	13.3
Transportation (most common form in the past month)	Pass. in a motor vehicle	18.2*	6.6	12.5**	43.5*	12.8	29.6	26.7*	8.5	17.9
	Public transit/ paratransit	7.9*	5.0	6.4	8.5*	4.9	6.9	8.1*	4.9	6.6
	Walking or cycling	3.6	3.5	3.6	4.0*	2.8	3.5	3.8	3.3	3.5
	Drive a motor vehicle	70.3*	85.0	77.5**	43.9*	79.5	60.1	61.5*	83.3	72.0
Retired	Yes	6.1*	7.4	6.7**	31.6*	38.4	35.8	7.7*	10.2	9.0
	No	93.9*	92.6	93.3**	68.4*	61.6	64.2	92.3*	89.8	91.0
Dwelling	Rent	17.1*	15.5	16.3**	28.9*	16.0	23.1	21.1*	15.7	18.5
	Own	82.9*	84.5	83.7**	71.1*	84.0	76.9	78.9*	84.3	81.5
Household income	Less than $20,000	7.9*	5.7	6.8**	23.1*	9.6	16.7	12.8*	6.9	9.8
	$20,000 - $39,999	14.9*	11.7	13.3**	37.0	36.1	36.6	22.0*	18.9	20.5
	$40,000 - $59,999	18.1*	16.3	17.2**	19.4*	23.2	21.2	18.5	18.3	18.4
	$60,000 - $79,999	18.4	18.5	18.4**	9.8*	12.6	11.2	15.7	16.8	16.2
	$80,000 and more	40.7*	47.9	44.3**	10.6*	18.5	14.3	31.0*	39.2	35.1
Immigrant	Yes	22.9	23.6	23.3**	25.9*	29.2	27.4	23.9*	25.3	24.6
	No	77.1	76.4	76.7**	74.1*	70.8	72.6	76.1*	74.7	75.4
Education	Less than secondary school	14.0	13.4	13.7**	44.1*	38.0	41.3	24.2*	20.9	22.6
	Secondary school	25.3*	18.4	21.9**	16.9*	13.6	15.4	22.4*	16.9	19.8
	Post-secondary	60.7*	68.2	64.4**	39.1*	48.4	43.3	53.4*	62.2	57.6
Chronic condition (at least one)	Yes	74.5*	68.4	71.5**	93.3*	88.9	91.3	80.8*	74.5	77.8
	No	25.5*	31.6	28.5**	6.7*	11.1	8.7	19.2*	25.5	22.2

	45-64			65 and over			Total		
	F	M	Total	F	M	Total	F	M	Total
Pain and discomfort	1.6 (1.1)*	1.5 (1.1)	1.5 (1.1)**	1.8 (1.3)*	1.6 (1.1)	1.7 (1.2)	1.6 (1.2)*	1.5 (1.1)	1.6 (1.1)
Mobility	1.1 (0.4)*	1.0 (0.3)	1.1 (0.3)**	1.4 (0.8)*	1.2 (0.7)	1.3 (0.8)	1.2 (0.6)*	1.1 (0.4)	1.1 (0.5)
Loneliness	3.9 (1.4)*	3.7 (1.3)	3.8 (1.4)**	3.9 (1.4)*	3.6 (1.2)	3.7 (1.3)	3.9 (1.4)*	3.7 (1.3)	3.8 (1.3)
Social support	13.2 (3.4)*	13.5 (3.4)	13.4 (3.4)	12.8 (3.8)*	13.9 (3.4)	13.3 (3.7)	13.0 (3.6)*	13.6 (3.4)	13.3 (3.5)

Scale values expressed as mean (standard deviation): *F and M are significantly different ($p < 0.01$) for each age group; **Age groups 45-64 and 65+ are significantly different ($p < 0.01$).

Similar low levels of pain and discomfort, mobility restrictions and loneliness were found across the country. Finally, social support was also about the same across the regions, with the exception of Quebec and the Atlantic region, where social support was marginally higher.

Canadians participated in an average of 12.8 activities per month (Table 3). For both age groups, women had slightly more community activities than men, with a few exceptions such as sports and physical activities. However, the most frequent types of activities differed according to age group. On average Canadians aged 65 and over participated more in church and religious activities, while younger ones tended to participate more in sports and physical, educational and cultural activities.

Regional distributions of community activities revealed a contrasting picture between Quebec's lower frequencies and the Prairies' higher frequencies (Table 4; Figure 1), with a minimum of 11.5 activities per month for men in Quebec and a maximum of 14.4 for women in Saskatchewan (data not shown). Activity frequencies were higher in the western and eastern regions, and somewhat weaker in Ontario and Quebec. The Atlantic region and Quebec showed the biggest differences between genders (differences respectively of 1.2 and 0.9 between women and men), while the gender differences in total monthly community activities were smaller in the other three regions (Table 4). For all regions, the three most frequent community activities were family or friends, church or religious, and sports or physical activities. However, church or religious activities showed the largest differences between regions, specifically between the highest levels in the Atlantic region and the lowest in Quebec.

Table 2. Sociodemographic characteristics of the population by Canadian region and gender (% and mean)

		Atlantic			Quebec			Ontario			Prairies			British Columbia		
		F	M	Total	F	M	Total	F	M	Total	F	M	Total	F	M	Total
Marital status	Married/Common-law	69.6*	80.9	75.0[a]	65.2*	77.9	71.3[b]	66.6*	81.8	73.9[a]	69.3*	81.0	75.0[a]	70.3*	81.1	75.5[a]
	Widowed	16.8*	4.3	10.8[a]	14.6*	3.5	9.3[a]	16.5*	4.2	10.6[a]	15.0*	3.7	9.5[a]	13.5*	4.5	9.1[a]
	Divorced/Separated	9.0	7.3	8.2[a]	11.6	10.8	11.2[b]	11.1*	7.8	9.5[ac]	10.0	8.3	9.2[ac]	12.4*	9.1	10.8[bc]
	Single	4.6*	7.5	6.0[ac]	8.6	7.7	8.2[b]	5.9	6.2	6.0[a]	5.7	7.0	6.3[a]	3.8	5.3	4.5[c]
Driver's license	Yes	80.7*	93.1	86.7[a]	77.3*	92.6	84.6[a]	78.2*	92.9	85.2[a]	87.2*	95.1	91.1[b]	84.1*	95.4	89.6[b]
	No	19.3*	6.9	13.3[a]	22.7*	7.4	15.4[a]	21.8*	7.1	14.8[a]	12.8*	4.9	8.9[b]	15.9*	4.6	10.4[b]
Transportation (most common form in the past month)	Pass. in a motor vehicle	33.1*	14.3	24.1[a]	28.7*	9.0	19.3[b]	26.0*	7.3	17.0[c]	26.2*	8.7	17.6[bc]	21.7*	7.2	14.6[d]
	Pub. transit, paratransit	2.7*	1.2	2.0[a]	9.8*	5.9	7.9[b]	9.4*	5.6	7.5[bd]	5.2	3.8	4.5[c]	7.7*	4.8	6.3[d]
	Walking or cycling	2.1	2.5	2.3[a]	4.3*	3.1	3.7[b]	3.7	3.5	3.6[ab]	3.3	3.5	3.4[ab]	4.5	3.1	3.8[b]
	Drive a motor vehicle	62.2*	82.0	71.7[abc]	57.2*	82.0	69.0[a]	61.0*	83.6	71.8[b]	65.3*	84.0	74.5[c]	66.1*	84.9	75.2[cd]
Retired	Yes	6.8	10.4	8.7[abc]	5.1*	7.9	6.6[a]	7.1*	10.6	8.9[b]	10.5	11.6	11.1[c]	10.5	10.9	10.7[bcd]
	No	93.2	89.6	91.3[abc]	94.9*	92.1	93.4[a]	92.9*	89.4	91.1[b]	89.5	88.4	88.9[c]	89.5	89.1	89.3[bcd]
Dwelling	Rent	16.5*	12.5	14.6[a]	29.9*	20.5	25.4[b]	20.4*	15.5	18.0[c]	15.0	12.7	13.9[a]	16.6*	12.8	14.8[a]
	Own	83.5*	87.5	85.4[a]	70.1*	79.5	74.6[b]	79.6*	84.5	82.0[c]	85.0	87.3	86.1[a]	83.4*	87.2	85.2[a]
Household income	Less than $20,000	16.0*	9.8	12.9[a]	15.9*	8.8	12.4[a]	11.5*	6.2	8.9[b]	10.5*	5.3	7.8[b]	11.3*	5.1	8.2[b]
	$20,000 - $39,999	27.0	27.2	27.1[a]	25.2	23.0	24.1[a]	20.6*	16.3	18.5[b]	19.0*	14.6	16.8[b]	20.4	18.5	19.5[b]
	$40,000 - $59,999	22.4	21.3	21.9[a]	19.9	19.0	19.5[ab]	17.6	18.5	18.0[bd]	17.8	17.0	17.4[bcd]	17.3	16.1	16.7[d]
	$60,000 - $79,999	13.0	16.5	14.7[ab]	16.2	18.3	17.2[a]	17.5	16.8	17.1[a]	13.4	15.9	14.7[b]	13.6	15.1	14.3[bc]
	$80,000 and more	21.6	25.2	23.4[a]	22.8*	30.9	26.8[a]	32.9*	42.2	37.5[b]	39.2*	47.2	43.3[c]	37.4*	45.3	41.3[c]
Immigrant	Yes	3.7	2.3	3.1[a]	10.9	10.5	10.7[b]	35.6	37.3	36.4[c]	16.2	18.5	17.3[d]	34.5*	38.9	36.7[c]
	No	96.3	97.7	96.9[a]	89.1	89.5	89.3[b]	64.4	62.7	63.6[c]	83.8	81.5	82.7[d]	65.5*	61.1	63.3[c]
Education	Less than secondary school	29.2	30.4	29.8[a]	32.4*	25.6	29.2[a]	22.1*	19.0	20.7[b]	20.2	19.4	19.8[b]	16.6	13.9	15.3[c]
	Secondary school	16.9	13.4	15.2[a]	19.3*	14.8	17.1[a]	24.7*	18.2	21.6[b]	21.3*	17.9	19.6[b]	26.3*	18.0	22.2[b]
	Post-secondary	53.9	56.3	55.0[ab]	48.3*	59.5	53.6[a]	53.2*	62.7	57.7[b]	58.5*	62.7	60.5[c]	57.2*	68.1	62.5[c]
Chronic condition (at least one)	Yes	84.7*	79.4	82.2[a]	78.8*	73.3	76.2[b]	81.4*	74.5	78.1[bc]	81.8*	76.8	79.4[ac]	79.5*	71.6	75.7[b]
	No	15.3*	20.6	17.8[a]	21.2*	26.7	23.8[b]	18.6*	25.5	21.9[bc]	18.2*	23.2	20.6[ac]	20.5*	28.4	24.3[b]

	Atlantic			Quebec			Ontario			Prairies			British Columbia		
	F	M	Total	F	M	Total	F	M	Total	F	M	Total	F	M	Total
Pain and discomfort	1.6 (1.2)	1.6 (1.2)	1.6 (1.2)^{a}	1.5 (1.0)*	1.4 (1.0)	1.5 (1.0)^{b}	1.7 (1.3)*	1.5 (1.1)	1.6 (1.2)^{a}	1.7 (1.2)*	1.5 (1.1)	1.6 (1.2)^{a}	1.7 (1.2)*	1.5 (1.1)	1.6 (1.2)^{a}
Mobility	1.2 (0.6)	1.1 (0.5)	1.1 (0.6)^{ab}	1.1 (0.6)*	1.1 (0.4)	1.1 (0.5)^{a}	1.2 (0.6)*	1.1 (0.5)	1.2 (0.6)^{b}	1.2 (0.6)*	1.1 (0.4)	1.1 (0.5)^{ab}	1.2 (0.6)*	1.1 (0.5)	1.1 (0.5)^{ab}
Loneliness	3.8 (1.4)*	3.6 (1.2)	3.7 (1.3)^{acd}	3.9 (1.3)*	3.6 (1.2)	3.7 (1.3)^{ab}	3.9 (1.4)*	3.7 (1.4)	3.8 (1.4)^{c}	3.9 (1.4)*	3.7 (1.3)	3.8 (1.3)	3.8 (1.4)^{acd}	3.7 (1.2)	3.7 (1.3)^{bd}
Social support	13.3 (3.3)*	13.8 (3.1)	13.5 (3.2)^{ab}	13.1 (3.5)*	13.9 (3.3)	13.5 (3.4)^{a}	13.0 (3.7)*	13.6 (3.5)	13.3 (3.6)^{bc}	13.0 (3.5)*	13.4 (3.7)	13.2 (3.6)^{c}	13.0 (3.5)*	13.6 (3.3)	13.3 (3.4)^{abc}

Scale values expressed as mean (standard deviation): *F and M are significantly different ($p < 0.01$) for each age group; **Region total and reference group (Quebec) are significantly different ($p < 0.01$); Note: Regions on the same row not sharing the same superscript are significantly different ($p < 0.01$).

Table 3. Monthly community activity frequencies according to gender and age

	45-64			65 and over			Total		
Activity	F	M	Total	F	M	Total	F	M	Total
Family/friends	3.9 (2.1)*	3.8 (2.2)	3.9 (2.2)	3.9 (2.3)	3.8 (2.3)	3.9 (2.3)	3.9 (2.2)*	3.8 (2.2)	3.9 (2.2)
Religious	1.7 (2.3)*	1.4 (2.2)	1.6 (2.3)**	2.5 (2.7)*	2.2 (2.6)	2.4 (2.7)	2.0 (2.5)*	1.7 (2.3)	1.8 (2.4)
Physical	2.4 (2.7)	2.4 (2.6)	2.4 (2.6)**	1.6 (2.6)*	1.9 (2.6)	1.7 (2.6)	2.1 (2.7)*	2.3 (2.6)	2.2 (2.6)
Educational	1.5 (1.7)*	1.3 (1.5)	1.4 (1.6)**	1.0 (1.5)	0.9 (1.5)	0.9 (1.5)	1.3 (1.7)*	1.2 (1.5)	1.2 (1.6)
Clubs	0.4 (1.2)	0.4 (1.2)	0.4 (1.2)**	0.7 (1.6)	0.7 (1.7)	0.7 (1.6)	0.5 (1.4)	0.5 (1.4)	0.5 (1.4)
Associations	0.7 (1.4)	0.7 (1.5)	0.7 (1.4)	0.8 (1.6)	0.7 (1.6)	0.8 (1.6)	0.7 (1.5)	0.7 (1.5)	0.7 (1.5)
Volunteering	1.2 (2.0)*	1.0 (1.8)	1.1 (1.9)	1.2 (2.1)	1.1 (2.0)	1.1 (2.1)	1.2 (2.0)*	1.0 (1.9)	1.1 (2.0)
Other recreational	1.2 (2.0)*	1.4 (2.0)	1.3 (2.0)**	1.5 (2.4)*	1.3 (2.2)	1.4 (2.3)	1.3 (2.1)	1.3 (2.1)	1.3 (2.1)
Total	13 (8.1)*	12.5 (8.1)	12.7 (8.1)	13.2 (9.2)	12.6 (8.8)	13.0 (9.0)	13.1 (8.5)*	12.5 (8.3)	12.8 (8.4)

Values expressed as mean (standard deviation): *F and M are significantly different ($p < 0.01$; t-test) for each age group; **Age groups 45-64 and 65+ are significantly different ($p < 0.01$; t-test).

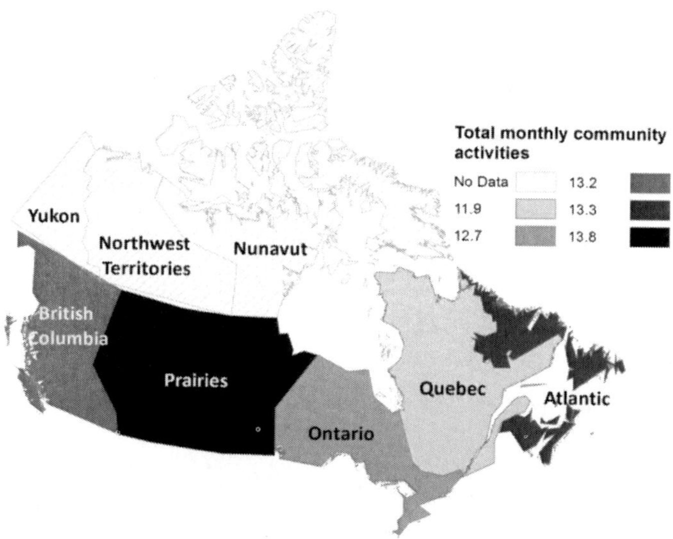

Figure 1. Spatial distribution of total monthly community activities by Canadian region, 2008-2009.

Figure 2. Spatial distribution of aging Canadians wanting to participate more.

Respondents living in a CMA participated in community activities similarly to those in a non-CMA (respectively 12.8 vs. 12.9; $p < 0.05$; data not shown in table). However, women living in a non-CMA were socially more active than men (13.4 vs. 12.5; $p < 0.05$). However, differences in participation in community activities were less clinically significant for women and men living in a CMA (12.9 vs. 12.6; $p < 0.05$; data not shown in table).

Regardless of gender, Canadians who had a driver's license participated on average in more community activities, particularly sports or physical activities, with a difference of more than one activity per month (Table 5). Men who did not have a driver's license seemed to be more restricted than those who had one, as their average total monthly community activities dropped by 4.7, versus 4.1 for women. Among those who participated least (six or less community activities per month; lowest quartile), half (50.1%) were men who did not have a valid driver's license (38.6% for women in the same situation; data not shown). If they had a driver's license, only 24.9% of men had six or less community activities per month (20.8% for women).

Table 4. Monthly community activity frequencies according to gender and Canadian region

	Atlantic			Quebec			Ontario			Prairies			British Columbia			Canada		
Activity	F	M	Total	F	M	Total	F	M	Total	F	M	Total	F	M	Total	F	M	Total
Family/friends	3.9 (2.2)*	3.6 (2.2)	3.7 (2.2)^a	3.7 (2.2)*	3.5 (2.2)	3.6 (2.2)^a	3.9 (2.2)	3.9 (2.2)	3.9 (2.2)^b	4.1 (2.1)*	4.0 (2.2)	4.1 (2.2)^c	4.2 (2.2)*	4.0 (2.2)	4.1 (2.2)^c	3.9 (2.2)*	3.8 (2.2)	3.9 (2.2)
Religious	2.5 (2.6)*	2.0 (2.5)	2.3 (2.6)^a	1.5 (2.2)	1.4 (2.1)	1.5 (2.1)^b	2.3 (2.6)*	1.8 (2.4)	2.1 (2.5)^c	2.1 (2.5)*	1.7 (2.4)	1.9 (2.5)^d	1.5 (2.4)	1.3 (2.3)	1.4 (2.3)^b	2.0 (2.5)*	1.7 (2.3)	1.8 (2.4)
Physical	2.0 (2.6)	2.0 (2.5)	2.0 (2.6)^a	2.3 (2.7)	2.3 (2.6)	2.3 (2.7)^b	1.9 (2.6)*	2.2 (2.6)	2.0 (2.6)^a	2.2 (2.6)*	2.5 (2.6)	2.3 (2.6)^{bc}	2.5 (2.4)	2.5 (2.6)	2.5 (2.7)^c	2.1 (2.7)*	2.3 (2.6)	2.2 (2.6)
Educational	1.1 (1.5)*	1.0 (1.4)	1.1 (1.4)^a	1.4 (1.9)*	1.2 (1.5)	1.3 (1.7)^b	1.2 (1.6)*	1.1 (1.5)	1.2 (1.6)^c	1.3 (1.5)	1.3 (1.4)	1.3 (1.5)^b	1.4 (1.6)	1.3 (1.5)	1.3 (1.6)^b	1.3 (1.7)*	1.2 (1.5)	1.2 (1.6)
Clubs	0.6 (1.4)	0.7 (1.6)	0.6 (1.5)^a	0.6 (1.5)	0.6 (1.4)	0.6 (1.4)^a	0.5 (1.3)	0.5 (1.3)	0.5 (1.3)^{bc}	0.5 (1.3)	0.6 (1.4)	0.5 (1.3)^{ab}	0.4 (1.2)	0.4 (1.3)	0.4 (1.3)^c	0.5 (1.4)	0.5 (1.4)	0.5 (1.4)
Associations	0.8 (1.5)	0.7 (1.5)	0.8 (1.5)^{ac}	0.6 (1.3)	0.5 (1.3)	0.6 (1.3)^b	0.7 (1.5)	0.8 (1.6)	0.7 (1.5)^a	0.9 (1.6)	0.9 (1.5)	0.9 (1.5)^c	0.9 (1.6)	0.8 (1.6)	0.8 (1.6)^{cd}	0.7 (1.5)	0.7 (1.5)	0.7 (1.5)
Volunteering	1.3 (2.0)	1.3 (2.1)	1.3 (2.0)^a	1.0 (1.9)*	0.9 (1.7)	0.9 (1.8)^b	1.1 (2.0)*	1.0 (1.9)	1.1 (2.0)^c	1.4 (2.0)*	1.2 (1.9)	1.3 (2.0)^a	1.3 (2.1)*	1.1 (2.0)	1.2 (2.1)^a	1.2 (2.0)*	1.0 (1.9)	1.1 (2.0)
Other recreational	1.7 (2.4)	1.5 (2.3)	1.6 (2.4)^a	1.2 (2.1)*	1.1 (1.9)	1.2 (2.0)^b	1.2 (2.1)*	1.3 (2.1)	1.3 (2.1)^c	1.5 (2.1)	1.6 (2.1)	1.5 (2.1)^a	1.3 (2.1)	1.5 (2.2)	1.4 (2.1)^c	1.3 (2.1)	1.3 (2.1)	1.3 (2.1)
Total	13.9 (8.7)*	12.7 (8.7)	13.3 (8.7)^{ac}	12.4 (8.3)*	11.5 (7.9)	11.9 (8.1)^b	12.9 (8.7)*	12.6 (8.5)	12.7 (8.6)^a	13.9 (8.3)	13.6 (8.6)	13.8 (8.4)^c	13.4 (8.1)*	12.9 (7.8)	13.2 (8.0)^{ac}	13.1 (8.5)*	12.5 (8.3)	12.8 (8.4)

Values expressed as mean (standard deviation): *F and M are significantly different ($p < 0.01$; t-test) for each age group; **Region total and reference group (Quebec) are significantly different ($p < 0.01$; t-test); Note: Regions on the same row not sharing the same superscript are significantly different ($p < 0.01$).

Table 5. Monthly community activity frequencies according to gender and driver's license

	Has a driver's license					
	Yes			No		
Activity	F	M	Total	F	M	Total
Family/friends	4.1 (2.1)*	3.8 (2.2)	4.0 (2.2)**	3.4 (2.3)*	3.1 (2.4)	3.3 (2.4)
Religious	1.9 (2.5)*	1.7 (2.3)	1.8 (2.4)**	2.1 (2.6)*	1.5 (2.4)	1.9 (2.5)
Physical	2.4 (2.7)	2.4 (2.6)	2.4 (2.7)**	1.0 (2.1)	0.9 (2.0)	1.0 (2.1)
Educational	1.5 (1.7)*	1.2 (1.5)	1.3 (1.6)**	0.7 (1.3)	0.5 (1.2)	0.6 (1.3)
Clubs	0.6 (1.4)	0.6 (1.4)	0.6 (1.4)**	0.3 (1.1)	0.3 (1.2)	0.3 (1.2)
Associations	0.8 (1.5)	0.8 (1.5)	0.8 (1.5)**	0.6 (1.5)	0.5 (1.4)	0.6 (1.5)
Volunteering	1.3 (2.1)*	1.1 (1.9)	1.2 (2.0)**	0.7 (1.7)*	0.4 (1.3)	0.6 (1.6)
Other recreational	1.4 (2.1)	1.4 (2.1)	1.4 (2.1)**	1.1 (2.1)	1.0 (2.0)	1.1 (2.1)
Total	13.9 (8.4)*	12.8 (8.3)	13.3 (8.4)**	9.8 (7.9)*	8.1 (7.1)	9.4 (7.8)

Values expressed as mean (standard deviation): *F and M are significantly different ($p < 0.01$; t-test); **Driver's License total and No Driver's License are significantly different ($p < 0.01$; t-test).

The younger respondents (45-64) wanted to participate more than the older (Table 6), but women in both age groups were more similar. The highest proportions of aging Canadians who wanted to participate more were in the western regions and Ontario (Figure 2). The eastern regions and especially Quebec showed the lowest proportions, with only one person in four wanting to participate more. Compared to those participating the most, a greater, but still modest, proportion of Canadians participating the least reported they wanted to be more involved (Table 7). Unlike women, men who did not want to participate more also mostly did not participate much.

Table 6. Older adults (%) reporting they want to participate more according to gender and age group

Want to participate more	45-64			65 and over			Total		
	F	M	Total	F	M	Total	F	M	Total
Yes	38.2*	35.3	36.8**	26.6*	20.7	23.9	34.3*	30.9	32.7
No	61.8*	64.7	63.2**	73.4*	79.3	76.1	65.7*	69.1	67.3

*F and M are significantly different ($p < 0.01$; t-test) for each age group; **Age groups 45-64 and 65+ are significantly different ($p < 0.01$; t-test).

Table 7. Older adults (%) in the lowest and highest quartiles of total monthly community activities according to gender, age and wanting to participate more

	Wanting to participate more																	
	Yes									No								
	45-64			65 and over			Total			45-64			65 and over			Total		
Quartile	F	M	Total	F	M	Total	F	M	Total	F	M	Total	F	M	Total	F	M	Total
Lowest	24.7	23.6	24.2	28.6	26.9	27.9	25.7	24.2	25.0	22.7	26.9	24.8	23.8	27.7	25.6	23.1	27.2	25.1
Highest	21.7	21.0	21.3	23.9	21.2	22.9	22.2	21.0	21.7	23.8	21.4	22.6	27.9	24.2	26.2	25.3	22.4	23.9

Table 8. Barriers to participating more according to age and gender (%)

	45-64			65 and over			Total		
Barriers	F	M	Total	F	M	Total	F	M	Total
Too busy	51.4*	54.8	53.0**	16.2*	28.4	20.9	42.3*	49.5	45.6
Health condition limitation	14.7*	12.2	13.5**	34.8	33.0	34.1	19.9*	16.4	18.3
Personal or family responsibilities	17.6*	11.1	14.6**	10.4	10.1	10.3	15.7*	10.9	13.6
Time of activities not suitable	*14.8*	*16.0*	*15.4***	*8.1*	*6.7*	*7.6*	*13.1*	*14.1*	*13.6*
Do not want to go alone	*12.6**	*6.7*	*9.9***	*16.7**	*9.0*	*13.7*	*13.7**	*7.2*	*10.8*
Cost	*12.0**	*9.4*	*10.8***	*8.6*	*7.5*	*8.2*	*11.1**	*9.0*	*10.2*
Activities not available in the area	*5.4*	*5.3*	*5.3***	*8.0*	*7.0*	*7.6*	*6.1*	*5.6*	*5.9*
Transportation problems	*4.3**	*1.5*	*3.0***	*11.2**	*3.7*	*8.3*	*6.1**	*1.9*	*4.2*
Location too far	*4.2*	*3.2*	*3.7***	*5.6*	*4.2*	*5.0*	*4.6**	*3.4*	*4.1*
Concerns about safety	*1.1**	*0.5*	*0.8***	*2.0*	*1.5*	*1.8*	*1.4**	*0.7*	*1.1*
Language barriers	*0.7*	*1.0*	*0.8***	*1.7*	*1.6*	*1.6*	*0.9*	*1.2*	*1.0*
Physical inaccessibility	*0.7*	*0.5*	*0.6***	*1.7*	*0.9*	*1.4*	*1.0*	*0.6*	*0.8*
Other	8.8*	10.7	9.7	8.9*	12.9	10.4	8.8*	11.1	9.9

*F and M are significantly different ($p < 0.01$; t-test) for each age group; **Age groups 45-64 and 65+ are significantly different ($p < 0.01$; t-test); In Italics: Environmental barriers.

Compared to the younger group and with the exception of health condition limitations, personal and environmental barriers became respectively less and more restrictive with respect to community activities in the older group (Table 8). Most environmental barriers restricted women more than men. Respondents not wanting to go alone, cost, and transportation problems were the most frequent environmental restrictions for more than one in ten women wanting to participate more. With the exception of cost, all environmental barriers were more restrictive for Canadians aged 65 and over.

For older Canadians living in non-CMAs, the non-availability of activities was a major barrier, even more for men than women (Table 9), in addition to transportation problems (10.6% of all women). With the exception of health condition limitations, personal barriers (too busy and personal or family responsibilities) were more important for aging Canadians living in a CMA.

Table 9. Barriers to participating more according to gender and location (%)

	CMA			Non-CMA		
Barriers	F	M	Total	F	M	Total
Too busy	17.2*	14.5	15.9**	25.4*	20.4	23.2
Health condition limitation	45.8*	52.2	48.7**	35.2*	43.9	39.1
Personal or family responsibilities	14.1*	7.3	11.0	12.8*	6.9	10.2
Time of activities not suitable	9.2*	12.4	10.7**	8.0	8.4	8.2
Do not want to go alone	17.2*	12.3	15.0**	12.8*	8.0	10.7
Cost	5.6*	1.8	3.9	7.0*	2.1	4.8
Activities not available in the area	5.3	4.2	4.8**	7.6	8.6	8.0
Transportation problems	14.4	13.4	13.9	10.6*	15.6	12.8
Location too far	4.1*	2.9	3.6**	5.4	4.6	5.1
Afraid or concerns about safety	1.5*	0.7	1.1	1.1	0.7	0.9
Language-related reasons	1.2	1.6	1.4**	0.3	0.3	0.3
Location not physically accessible	1.0*	0.2	0.7	0.9	1.2	1.0
Other	11.0*	8.6	9.9	11.4	10.0	10.8

*F and M are significantly different ($p < 0.01$; t-test); **CMA total and Non-CMA total are significantly different ($p < 0.01$; t-test); In Italics: Environmental barriers.

Finally, environmental barriers differed across Canadian regions. Non-availability of activities was a barrier for community activities for one in ten Canadian older women in the Atlantic and Prairies regions (Table 10). Also and unlike men, one in five women in the Prairies did not want to go alone to community activities. Health condition limitations, such as chronic conditions, were a barrier for more than one in four women in the Atlantic region.

Table 10. Barriers to participating more according to gender and Canadian region (%)

	Atlantic			Quebec			Ontario			Prairies			British Columbia		
Barriers	F	M	Total	F	M	Total	F	M	Total	F	M	Total	F	M	Total
Health condition limitation	26.7	22.3	24.8[a]	17.0	17.7	17.3[b]	19.4*	14.3	17.2[b]	19.9	15.2	17.7[b]	21.3	18.6	20.0[ab]
Too busy	32.0	40.5	35.7[a]	41.9*	48.5	44.8[b]	43.1*	52.5	47.3[b]	44.9*	51.5	48.0[b]	43.0	45.2	44.1[b]
Do not want to go alone	10.5*	4.9	8.0[a]	12.0*	5.7	9.3[a]	12.5*	7.7	10.4[ab]	20.2*	5.5	13.3[b]	13.2	10.5	11.9[ab]
Personal or family responsibilities	15.8*	8.1	12.5[acd]	12.5	9.4	11.2[ab]	16.7*	13.1	15.1[c]	14.2*	8.0	11.3[bd]	19.2*	12.1	15.7[ce]
Transportation problems	7.9*	2.0	5.3[a]	5.7*	1.1	3.8[a]	6.4*	2.5	4.7[a]	5.0*	1.3	3.3[a]	6.1*	1.9	4.1[a]
Cost	11.5*	4.7	8.5[ab]	10.6*	5.0	8.2[a]	11.6	11.2	11.4[b]	10.4	8.2	9.3[ab]	11.4	11.2	11.3[ab]
Activities not available in the area	10.1	7.9	9.1[a]	5.1	5.1	5.1[b]	4.6	4.8	4.7[b]	9.9	7.5	8.7[a]	4.9	5.1	5.0[b]
Time of activities not suitable	14.4	12.7	13.7[ab]	11.6*	17.0	13.9[ab]	11.5	12.1	11.8[a]	17.4	17.3	17.4[b]	13.5	12.9	13.2[ab]
Location too far	5.0	3.3	4.3[a]	3.4	3.2	3.3[a]	4.4*	2.8	3.7[a]	6.0	3.9	5.0[a]	4.6	4.8	4.7[a]
Afraid or concerns about safety	1.5	0.2	1.0[a]	0.8	0.4	0.6[a]	1.0	1.2	1.1[a]	2.7*	0.5	1.6[a]	1.6*	0.0	0.9[a]
Language-related reasons	0.4	0.1	0.3[a]	1.0	1.6	1.2[a]	0.9	1.1	1.0[a]	0.7	0.7	0.7[a]	1.5	1.7	1.6[a]
Location not physically accessible	1.2	0.7	1.0[a]	0.9	0.0	0.5[a]	1.1*	0.3	0.7[a]	0.8	1.4	1.1[a]	0.9	0.7	0.8[a]
Other	6.6	9.6	7.9[a]	8.2	9.5	8.7[a]	8.8*	12.2	10.3[a]	9.6	11.9	10.7[a]	9.9	10.3	10.1[a]

*F and M are significantly different ($p < 0.01$; t-test) for each Canadian region; **Region total and reference group (Quebec) are significantly different ($p < 0.01$; t-test). Note: Regions on the same row not sharing the same superscript are significantly different ($p < 0.01$). In Italics: Environmental barriers.

Discussion

This chapter aimed to describe and compare social participation and barriers among older Canadians according to gender, age and location. Results showed that social participation is influenced by individual and environmental characteristics, both of which can be addressed by public policies and explored more thoroughly in future research. The present discussion addresses issues raised by the results, especially concerning gender, transportation problems, environmental barriers and location.

As previously emphasized, no research on social participation should ignore gender differences (Shye, Mullooly, Freeborn & Pope, 1995) and the present study confirmed this. Older women tended to have slightly more monthly community activities than men, although both genders enjoyed roughly the same types of activities, which is consistent with previous studies (Gilmour, 2012; Lefrancois, Leclerc, Dubé, Hamel & Gaulin, 2001). Women, especially when they had less monthly community activities, wanted to participate more. More than one in four women felt that way. Such distributions warrant further exploration of restrictions to social participation.

Results showed that older Canadians, and women more significantly, who did not have a driver's license had less social participation, as previous studies have shown (Cao et al., 2010; Therrien & Desrosiers, 2010). This raises the issue of the availability of public transit for older Canadians living in rural areas, and also in urban areas where accessibility may be lacking. Poor access to public transportation, especially when one does not have a driver's license, is linked to lower social participation and functional loss (Balfour & Kaplan, 2002; Julien et al., 2014). Transportation problems may be a growing concern, as 25.1% of Canadians aged 65 and over did not have a driver's license (versus 7.8% of the 45-64 age group; Table 1). Since transportation problems were one of the most important environmental barriers, particularly for women, strategies aimed at improving social participation should explore this aspect. Canadian older women, no matter the age group, were also more restricted by environmental barriers. Given that older Canadian women are proportionally more numerous in the lowest quartiles of the income distribution (Denton, Prus & Walters, 2004), it is no surprise to see cost barriers are more prevalent among women than men. Costs are not the only issue of concern with respect to community activities. The timeframe in which these activities are held are not always convenient (for example, pool sessions for seniors only in the early morning). Adding non-availability and distance to activities, it seems that older Canadians are not completely satisfied with the potential for community activities in their local environment. Such barriers should guide public officials with respect to social participation challenges in the community. As community demographics change, the need for different types of community activities will probably evolve as well. Nevertheless, such barriers to increased social participation are consistent with studies showing that social participation is negatively correlated with an unfavorable environment (Glass & Balfour, 2003; Levasseur et al., 2015 Submitted).

Rural and urban environments were deemed different, as mentioned in the introduction, thus affecting social participation differently. However, comparing total monthly community activities of older adults living in a CMA or non-CMA showed only a small difference, as was also found by Therrien and Desrosiers (2010) and Levasseur et al. (In Press). Barriers to community activities, on the other hand, proved to be different between the two types of area, which has not been properly addressed in the literature. Availability of activities, for example, seemed to be a greater issue in non-CMAs. In addition to transportation problems and distance, especially for women, this suggests that a growing proportion of older Canadians living in non-CMAs will not be able to practice community activities they enjoy. Finally, spatial representation of monthly community activities revealed an unequal distribution between Canadian regions, showing that older adults did not take part in community activities with the same frequency. Subsequent results suggested that restrictions on increased participation were also different. Cost, for example, was an important limiting factor older adults, more so in Ontario and British Columbia. The same could be said about resource availability in the Prairies and Atlantic regions. Also, aging Atlantic Canadians reported higher proportions of chronic conditions, which is consistent with them being the most restricted by health condition limitations. These parallel distributions of demography, physical health and barriers point to the need to look more closely at local community and environment in future research.

Strengths and Limitations

This study increases our understanding of social participation of older Canadians living in different locations, and identifies the main environmental barriers to community activities. These results can help decision-makers consider their communities' challenges for the aging Canadian population. The large sample of 30,635 respondents from the 2008-2009 CCHS "Healthy Aging" thematic increased the representativeness of the study population,

Canadian older adults. This study has some limitations. While most monthly community activity frequencies were statistically different, such differences were not always clinically significant. Also, the publically available data were limited in terms of community activity frequency options, making it impossible to differentiate between daily and weekly activities. Also, the classification between CMA and non-CMA was used only as a proxy to explore the rural / urban divide. Rural areas can be found in CMAs. However, considering Statistics Canada's definition of a CMA (2010b), even these rural areas are in a close relationship with dense urban areas.

CONCLUSION

This chapter's objectives were to describe and compare prevalence and patterns of social participation among older Canadians from the 2008-2009 CCSH data. The analysis suggests that demography and geography are important factors influencing social participation among older Canadians. The location of the survey respondents seems to be an important factor that should be considered in future investigations. Public health efforts to increase older adults' social participation must be localized, if they are to be efficient. As discussed, the region of residence and the type of area one lives in have an impact on community activities and barriers to a full and rewarding social life.

This study was an exploration of the CCSH's publically available data. Future research will explore the CCSH's micro data, allowing the researchers to analyze in more depth environmental factors influencing older Canadians' social participation. Some knowledge derived from the present results can be transferred to future analyses, such as the distribution of environmental barriers among older Canadians, as well as gender. Paying closer attention to respondents' locations will improve our understanding of the relationship between social participation and local environment. Future research will ultimately help guide policy and planning strategies.

REFERENCES

Adams, K. B., Leibbrandt, S., & Moon, H. (2011). A critical review of the literature on social and leisure activity and wellbeing in later life. *Ageing and Society,* 31(04), 683-712.

Balfour, J. L., & Kaplan, G. A. (2002). Neighborhood environment and loss of physical function in older adults: evidence from the Alameda County Study. *American Journal of Epidemiology,* 155(6), 507-515.

Canadian Institute for Health Information (2011). *Seniors and the Health Care System: What Is the Impact of Multiple Chronic Conditions?* Ottawa, ON: CIHI.

Cao, X., Mokhtarian, P. L., & Handy, S. L. (2010). Neighborhood design and the accessibility of the elderly: An empirical analysis in Northern California. *International Journal of Sustainable Transportation,* 4(6), 347-371.

Davison, K. K., & Lawson, C. T. (2006). Do attributes in the physical environment influence children's physical activity? A review of the literature. *International Journal of Behavioral Nutrition and Physical Activity,* 3(1), 19.

De Leon, C. F. M., Glass, T. A., & Berkman, L. F. (2003). Social engagement and disability in a community population of older adults: the New Haven EPESE. *American Journal of Epidemiology,* 157(7), 633-642.

Denton, M., Prus, S., & Walters, V. (2004). Gender differences in health: a Canadian study of the psychosocial, structural and behavioural determinants of health. *Social Science & Medicine,* 58(12), 2585-2600.

Desrosiers, J., Noreau, L., & Rochette, A. (2004). Social participation of older adults in Quebec. *Aging Clinical and Experimental Research,* 16(5), 406-412.

Engelhardt, H., Buber, I., Skirbekk, V., & Prskawetz, A. (2010). Social involvement, behavioural risks and cognitive functioning among older people. *Ageing and Society,* 30(05), 779-809.

ESRI (2011). *ArcGIS Desktop: Release 10.1.* Redlands, CA: Environmental Systems Research Institute.

Fiori, K. L., Antonucci, T. C., & Cortina, K. S. (2006). Social network typologies and mental health among older adults. *The Journals of Gerontology Series B: Psychological Sciences and Social Sciences,* 61(1), P25-P32.

Gilmour, H. (2012). *Social participation and the health and well-being of Canadian seniors.* Cat. No. 82-003-x, Vol. 23. No. 4. Ottawa, ON: Statistics Canada.

Glass, T. A., & Balfour, J. L. (2003). Neighborhoods, aging, and functional limitations. *Neighborhoods and Health,* 303-334.

Glass, T. A., De Leon, C. F. M., Bassuk, S. S., & Berkman, L. F. (2006). Social engagement and depressive symptoms in late life longitudinal findings. *Journal of Aging and Health,* 18(4), 604-628.

Heyden, G. (1998). Health profile of the ageing population: the Swedish experience. *International Dental Journal,* 48(3), 167-172.

Hughes, M. E., Waite, L. J., Hawkley, L. C., & Cacioppo, J. T. (2004). A short scale for measuring loneliness in large surveys results from two population-based studies. *Research on Aging,* 26(6), 655-672.

Julien, D., Richard, L., Gauvin, L., Fournier, M., Kestens, Y., Shatenstein, B., &Payette, H. (2014). Transit use and walking as potential mediators of the association between accessibility to services and amenities and social participation among urban-dwelling older adults: Insights from the VoisiNuAge study. *Journal of Transport & Health.*

Lawton, M. P. (1986). *Environment and aging,* 2nd ed. Monterey, CA: Brooks/Cole.

Lebel, A., & Charbonneau, P. (2014). *Annual Demographic Estimates: Canada, Provinces and Territories.* Ottawa, ON: Statistics Canada. Retrieved from http://www.statcan.gc.ca/pub/91-215-x/91-215-x2014000-eng. htm.

Lefrancois, R., Leclerc, G., Dubé, M., Hamel, S., & Gaulin, P. (2001). Valued activities of everyday life among the very old: A one-year trend. *Activities, Adaptation & Aging,* 25(3-4), 19-34.

Levasseur, M., Cohen, A. A., Dubois, M.-F., Généreux, M., Richard, L., Therrien, F.-H., & Payette, H. (In Press). Environmental Factors Associated With Social Participation of Older Adults Living in Metropolitan, Urban, and Rural Areas: The NuAge Study. *American Journal of Public Health.*

Levasseur, M., Généreux, M., Bruneau, J.-F., Vanasse, A., Chabot, É., Beaulac, C., & Bédard, M.-M. (2015 Submitted). Importance of Proximity to resources and to recreational facilities, Social support, Transportation and Neighborhood security for mobility and social participation in older adults: Results from a scoping study. *BMC Public Health.*

Levasseur, M., Richard, L., Gauvin, L., & Raymond, E. (2010). Inventory and analysis of definitions of social participation found in the aging literature: proposed taxonomy of social activities. *Social Science & Medicine,* 71 (12), 2141-2149.

Li, Y., & Ferraro, K. F. (2005). Volunteering and depression in later life: Social benefit or selection processes? *Journal of Health and Social Behavior,* 46(1), 68-84.

Lund, R., Nilsson, C. J., & Avlund, K. (2010). Can the higher risk of disability onset among older people who live alone be alleviated by strong social relations? A longitudinal study of non-disabled men and women. *Age and Ageing,* 39(3), 319-326.

Marmot, M., Friel, S., Bell, R., Houweling, T. A., & Taylor, S. (2008). Closing the gap in a generation: Health equity through action on the social determinants of health. *The Lancet,* 372(9650), 1661-1669.

McDaniel, S. A., & Rozanova, J. (2011). Canada's Aging Population (1986) Redux. *Canadian Journal on Aging,* 30(03), 511-521. doi:10.1017/s 0714 980811000420

Richard, L., Gauvin, L., Gosselin, C., & Laforest, S. (2009). Staying connected: Neighbourhood correlates of social participation among older adults living in an urban environment in Montreal, Quebec. *Health Promotion International,* 24(1), 46-57.

Richard, L., Gauvin, L., Kestens, Y., Shatenstein, B., Payette, H., Daniel, M., Mercille, G. (2012). Neighborhood resources and social participation among older adults: Results from the VoisiNuage Study. *Journal of Aging and Health,* 25(2), 296-318.

Seeman, T. E. (2000). Health promoting effects of friends and family on health outcomes in older adults. *American Journal of Health Promotion,* 14(6), 362-370.

Shye, D., Mullooly, J. P., Freeborn, D. K., & Pope, C. R. (1995). Gender differences in the relationship between social network support and mortality: a longitudinal study of an elderly cohort. *Social Science & Medicine,* 41(7), 935-947.

SPSS Inc. (2008). *SPSS Statistics for Windows, Version 17.0.* Chicago, IL: SPSS.

Statistics Canada (2008-2009). *Canadian Community Health Survey (2008-2009): Healthy Aging*. (Machine readable data file).

Statistics Canada (2010a). *Canadian Community Health Survey (CCHS): Healthy Aging:* Approximate Sampling Variability Tables. Ottawa, ON: Statistics Canada.

Statistics Canada (2010b). *Census Metropolitan Area and Census Agglomeration definitions*. Ottawa, ON: Statistics Canada. Retrieved from http://www.statcan.gc.ca/pub/93-600-x/2010000/definitions-eng.htm.

Therrien, F. H., & Desrosiers, J. (2010). Participation of metropolitan, urban and rural community-dwelling older adults. *Archives of Gerontology and Geriatrics,* 51(3), e52-56.

United Nations (2000). *Replacement migration: Is it a solution to declining and ageing populations?* New York, NY: United Nations.

Valtorta, N., & Hanratty, B. (2012). Loneliness, isolation and the health of older adults: do we need a new research agenda? *Journal of the Royal Society of Medicine,* 105(12), 518-522.

Walsh, D., McCartney, G., McCullough, S., van der Pol, M., Buchanan, D., & Jones, R. (2013). *Exploring potential reasons for Glasgow's 'excess' mortality:* Results of a three-city survey of Glasgow, Liverpool and Manchester. Glasgow, UK: Glasgow Centre for Population Health.

Webber, S. C., Porter, M. M., & Menec, V. H. (2010). Mobility in older adults: a comprehensive framework. *The Gerontologist*, gnq013.

Wilkins, K. (2003). Social support and mortality in seniors. *Health Reports* (Vol. 14(3)). Ottawa, ON: Statistics Canada.

In: Social Isolation, Participation …
Editor: Kristin T. Rowe
ISBN: 978-1-63482-505-4

Chapter 2

SOCIAL ISOLATION AND PSYCHOLOGICAL ADJUSTMENT AMONG EARLY ADOLESCENT IMMIGRANTS

Jacqueline Oxman-Martinez[1], PhD and Ye Ri Choi[2],
[1]School of Social Work, University of Montreal, Canada
[2]School of Social Work, McGill University, Canada

ABSTRACT

The present chapter examines the influence of potential social isolation factors on the psychological outcomes of immigrant youth in early adolescent. Data are derived from the New Canadian Children and Youth Study (NCCYS), a national longitudinal survey including 459 immigrant youth aged 11 to 13 years living in the Greater Montreal region, Canada from five ethnic groups (Mainland China, Hong Kong, the Philippines, Haiti, and Lebanon). Four social isolation factors in relation to peers are included as predictors: perceived peer rejection based on ethnic background, feelings of disconnectedness from others, perceived relationships with peers, and the absence of close friendships. Self-esteem and emotional distress are included as psychological outcomes. Multivariate analyses are performed to examine the effects of the social isolation factors on self-esteem and emotional distress of immigrant youth. The results show that peer rejection based on ethnic background, feelings of disconnectedness, and perceived relationships with peers are significantly associated with self-esteem and emotional distress, after controlling for demographic background variables. Significant variations across ethnic groups are also found in feelings of disconnectedness from others, the absence of close friendships, perceived relationships with peers, and emotional distress. These findings suggest that social isolation experiences in relation to peer interactions are critical factors affecting self-esteem and emotional distress of early adolescent immigrants. The findings and implications are discussed with respect to the social contexts of the lives of immigrant youth and migration-related issues.

INTRODUCTION

Social relationships have been considered an important challenge for individuals beginning in childhood and running across the life course (Hay, Payne, & Chadwick, 2004; Hartup & Stevens, 1997). Social isolation and loneliness take place within the social relational context. It has been well documented that during childhood and adolescence, forming meaningful peer relationships have predicted positive well-being, while difficulties in establishing satisfactory peer relationships have been linked to adverse outcomes (Asher & Paquette, 2003; Gest, 1997; Hall-Lande, Eisenberg, Christenson, & Neumark-Sztainer, 2007; Laursen, Bukowski, Aunola, & Nurmi, 2007: Qualter, Brown, Munn, & Rotenberg, 2010). Social isolation also emerges from negative peer experiences such as peer rejection, victimization, and discrimination, resulting in increased maladjustment (Hymel, Vaillancourt, McDougall, & Renshaw, 2002; Omidvar & Richmond, 2003; Rubin & Burgess, 2001). Thus the quality of interpersonal connections with peers may be considered as a significant indicator of social isolation affecting developmental adjustment. To date, most studies of social isolation and peer relationships have tended to focus on ethnical majority children in relatively ethnically homogeneous settings (e.g., Hay, Payne, & Chadwick, 2004). The present chapter, therefore, attempts to explore the experiences of immigrant youth in relation to social isolation and social relationships with peers, accounting for the ethnic heterogeneity.

It is important to examine social isolation from a developmental perspective. We particularly focus on youth in early adolescence. This transitional period represents a sequence of two developmental stages that occur at the threshold of adolescence. It is a uniquely awkward developmental stage that somehow bridges the gap between childhood and adolescence (Broderick & Blewitt, 2006; Wiles, Bondi, & Wiles, 2006). New social interactions and pressure are indicative that individuals strive towards independence from the parents and towards close peer relationships. Through gradual developmental changes involving the physical, intellectual and social life of youth, the well-knit pattern of childhood personality is considerably loosened as youth experience identifying behaviours with other youth, and thus move toward adolescence.

For immigrant youth, along with normal maturational changes, this transitional period is a particularly difficult time with acculturation and adaptation processes. According to the report conducted by Ontario Council of Agencies Serving Immigrants (OCASI, 2009), newcomer immigrant youth tend to suffer from social isolation in the absence of the social and support networks that they had in their homeland. They also may struggle to connect to their peers when they try to forge friendships in their new environment due to lack of language proficiency, different cultural behaviours, and ethnic discrimination (Fuligni, 2004; Ngo & Schleifer, 2005; Omidvar & Richmond, 2003). Migration-related stresses seem to be critical factors that contribute to immigrant youth's social relationships with peers and psychological distress.

We first explore the potential social isolation factors affecting the psychological outcomes of immigrant youth. The following four factors are used as indexes of social isolation in relation to peer experiences: perceived peer rejection based on ethnic background, feelings of disconnectedness from others at school, perceived relationships with peers, and the absence of close friendships. First, perceived peer rejection based on ethnic background is operationalized as a perception of peer discrimination/ peer victimization on the basis of differences in appearance, skin colour, accent, or being born outside of Canada. Second, feelings of disconnectedness from others describe the negative experiences of psychological isolation or exclusion at school (the immigrant adolescent feels like an outsider or left out of things at school). The last two factors describe the peer relationships of immigrant youth; perceived relationships with peers assess the peer relationships *in general*, whereas the absence of close friendships measures *the quality* of peer relationships. The current chapter also examines if the prevalence of social isolation and psychological outcomes vary across ethnic groups. Finally, it aims to determine whether social isolation factors have significant associations with self-esteem and emotional distress among early adolescent immigrants.

Study Background and Literature Review

Peer Experiences, Social Isolation and Psychological Adjustment

The most controversial change during early adolescence may be the youth's increasing focus on peers. Many early adolescents give priority to social activities with peers and peer acceptance (Wigfield, Eccles, Maclver et al., 1991). Peer relationships often provide practice of interpersonal connections with opportunities to learn social interaction and problem-solving skills. These social relations are important sources of self-knowledge and self-esteem that enable the development of social competence (Waldrip, Malcolm, & Jensen-Campbell, 2008). Since early adolescence is a time of increased need for social and emotional connections with peers, social isolation in this developmental stage can be characterized by the lack of close relationships with peers. Previous research indicated that positive peer interactions serve as buffers to loneliness, and as bolsterers of self-confidence and self-efficacy providing emotional sustenance (Suarez-Orozco, Suarez-Orozco, & Todorova, 2008; Gibson, Gandara, & Koyama, 2004; Way & Phal, 2001). In contrast, being friendless tends to influence negatively psychological adjustment; early adolescents who lack mutual friends reported higher levels of loneliness and internalizing problems than those with friends (Rubin, Fredstrom, & Bowker, 2008). Social isolation may emerge not only from the absence of peer relationships, but also from negative experiences in peer relational contexts such as social exclusion from peer groups and peer victimization. Previous studies indicate that peer rejection and victimization have been associated with a range of harmful psychological consequences including low self-esteem, social anxiety, and depression (Boivin, Hymel, & Bukowski, 1995; Hymel, Vaillancourt, McDougall, & Renshaw, 2002; Juvonen, & Graham, 2001). Since immigrant youth often experience profound shifts in their sense of self and struggle to negotiate changing circumstances in their social worlds (Rhodes, 2002), coping with additional unique adjustment processes as well as normal developmental changes is a major task for early adolescent immigrants.

The Effects of Migration and Ethnicity on Peer Experiences and Social Isolation

It is generally argued that immigrant youth are at risk for social adjustment problems in their new social settings such as schools. Social experiences in peer groups can be a significant source of stress. Through peer interactions, immigrant youth face challenges and difficulties that are related to their immigrant status and ethnicities such as differences in cultural norms on social behaviours, language barriers, and biased or prejudiced attitudes. Since schools are the most critical arena in which immigrant youth's major social interactions occur with profound consequences for their developmental adjustment, our study includes a sense of isolation/ exclusion at school (feelings of disconnectedness from others at school) as an index of social isolation.

After migration, immigrant youth who were socialized under different cultural societies may experience difficulties in social interactions because their behavioural styles are perceived differently by other peers in a new host society. Particular social behaviour styles that are accepted in the country of origin may no longer be viewed as adaptive or appropriate by peers in a host society (Way, 2006; Zhou, Perverly, Xin, Huang, & Wang, 2003). For instance, shy and withdrawn characteristics have diverse implications in different cultures. Youth with shyness and withdrawn behaviours are regarded in Western cultures as socially incompetent and immature (Fox, Henderson, Marshall, Nichols, & Ghera, 2005; Rubin et al., 2009). Thus shy immigrant youth tend to experience problems in peer interactions that contribute to the feelings of social isolation, loneliness (Chen et al., 2004), and peer rejection or victimization (e.g., Ladd, 2006; Rubin et al, 1995). Therefore the different expectations of social behaviours may have significantly negative effects on social relationships of immigrant youth which, in turn, lead to psychological distress. Language proficiency also plays a critical role in peer interactions of immigrant youth. Immigrant youth often encounter language obstacles in the transition to a new host society during acculturation and adaptation processes that may undermine their abilities to display competent behaviours in social interactions and obtain peer acceptance (e.g., Von Grunigen, Kochenderfer-Ladd, Perren, & Alsaker; 2012). Briefly, immigrant youth who have difficulty communicating with their peers may be more likely to withdraw from social interactions, thereby leaving them vulnerable to poor peer relationships.

With regard to perceived peer rejection based on ethnic background used as an index of social isolation in the current study, immigrant youth may be subjected to ethnic victimization, contributing to feelings of exclusion and alienation (Cooper, McLoyd, Wood, & Hardaway, 2008; Garcia-Coll & Szalacha, 2004). Verkuyten et al. (1997) refer specifically to those situations where negative peer experiences are related to children's ethnic group membership. Our study focuses on *ethnic* victimization based on one's ethnic background rather than *personal* victimization. Peer victimization can be identified in two types of bullying: direct and indirect (relational) behaviour forms (Woods, Done, & Kalsi, 2009). The former refers to physically aggressive acts such as kicking, pushing, and hitting, while the latter refers to name calling, teasing, socially isolating others, and spreading false rumors. Previous research findings consistently showed high levels of ethnic-based peer victimization and discrimination toward immigrant youth (Alvarez, Juang, & Liang, 2006; Fisher, Wallace, & Fenton, 2000; Greene, Way, & Phal, 2006; Grossman & Liang, 2008). The experience of ethnic-based peer rejection may serve to exacerbate immigrant youth's social adjustment difficulties.

STUDY OBJECTIVES AND RESEARCH QUESTIONS

Much previous research has identified significant aspects of social isolation that contribute to adolescents' psychological health. However, there has been sparse research attention to the importance of further understanding of social isolation among immigrant adolescents in particular during early adolescence whose experiences and perceptions may be different from other groups. This chapter seeks to fulfill this gap. The inclusion of diverse immigrant groups considering ethnic heterogeneity also provides a more broad view of social isolation experienced by immigrant youth.

Our study purpose is three-fold. First, it explores the potential social isolation factors in relation to peer experiences of immigrant youth in early adolescence: a) perceived peer rejection based on ethnic background, b) feelings of disconnectedness from others, c) perceived relationships with peers, and, d) the absence of close friendships. Second, it examines whether the prevalence of social isolation and psychological adjustment outcomes vary across ethnic groups. Lastly, it examines the effects of social isolation factors on psychological adjustment of immigrant youth. In particular, the following research questions are addressed: 1) what are the possible social isolation factors involved in early adolescent immigrants' psychological adjustment?; 2) are there variations in the levels of the potential predictors of social isolation and immigrant youth outcomes across ethnic groups?; and 3) are there significant associations between social isolation factors and psychological adjustment outcomes (self-esteem and emotional distress)?

METHODS

Data and Sampling

The primary data used in the present study are drawn from the New Canadian Children and Youth Study (NCCYS), a national longitudinal survey of the health and well-being of approximately 4,000 immigrant children living in Montreal, Toronto, the Prairies (Winnipeg, Edmonton, Calgary), and Vancouver, Canada (Beiser et al., 2010). Children participating in the survey of the NCCYS project were either foreign-born or Canadian-born into families in which at least one parent had immigrated to Canada during the ten years preceding the study's beginnings. They were also in one of two age-defined inception cohorts (the border of important developmental transitions): children 4-6 years and children 11-13 years old.

Our research focuses on early adolescents -11 to 13 years of age, including a sub-sample of the full survey with 459 early adolescents and their families residing in the Greater Montreal area, Quebec, Canada from five source countries: Mainland China (117), Hong Kong (86), the Philippines (80), Haiti (85), and Lebanon (91). Three Asian groups (Mainland China, Hong Kong, and the Philippines) are the national-level samples of the NCCYS. These groups were chosen because, during the decades preceding the initiation of the NCCYS, they were the leading source countries for Canadian immigration (Citizenship & Immigration Canada, 2006). Haitian and Lebanese groups are the Montreal regional-level samples of the NCCYS. They represented the largest visible ethnic groups whose second language is French, the Quebec official language. From the sample of this study, the majority (84.0%) of the children were foreign-born with a mean of 5.5 years, length of time in Canada, while only 16.0% were born in Canada.

The NCCYS employed respondent-driven snowball strategies to identify hard-to-reach and highly mobile immigrant populations. Local community organizations were contacted about the study, and formal invitations to participate in the study were extended to family members who had initially provided verbal consent to participate. Bilingual interviewers who spoke the language of origin and one or the other official language (French or English) were recruited from these same community groups. The interviewers were trained in survey interviewing by the researchers. The researchers of the study provided interviewers with a list of the names and phone numbers of potential respondents. Interviewers contacted the families by telephone to arrange an appointment to conduct the interviews with families who fit NCCYS inclusion criteria in terms of length of time in Canada (less than 10 years) and age cohort (11-13 years old). During the household visit, interviewers explained the study, obtained written informed consent, and collected data with the questionnaires.

Questionnaires and Measurements

The study instruments consisted of five questionnaires developed by the New Canadian Children and Youth Study (NCCYS) and the National Longitudinal Survey of Children and Youth (NLSCY): Demographic Information (DI), Parent about Family (PAF), Parent about Child (PAC), Child about Child (CAC), and Child Identity (CI) (Beiser et al., 2010). All questionnaires were translated from English to French and then into each of the heritage languages (i.e., Mandarin, Cantonese, Tagalog, Creole, and Lebanese Arabic). Standard back- translation procedures were utilized to ensure cultural equivalence of concepts in the different languages of the study. The project team consulted with the specifically formed Ethno-cultural Community Advisory Councils for the appropriateness of questions as well as language.

The informants for the study included both youth in early adolescence and the PMK (Person Most Knowledgeable about the child). The vast majority of the PMKs were biological mothers. Parents were able to review the Child about Child (CAC) questionnaire before the questionnaire was filled out by the child. To ensure privacy for children's responses, the children's questionnaire was given to the interviewer in a sealed envelope upon completion.

The variables used in the current study were drawn from the following questionnaires: Demographic Information and Parent about Family reported by PMK; and Child about Child reported by the adolescent.

Dependent Variables

The dependent variables of psychological outcomes included self-esteem and emotional distress. The self-esteem measure (derived from the CAC) is a sub-scale of the General-Self Scale of the Marsh Self-Description

Questionnaire developed by Marsh (1988). It includes four items with four response choices from 0.never to 3.most of the time that aim to measure an adolescent's overall self-esteem: a) I like the way I am; b) I have a lot to be proud of; c) a lot of things about me are good; and d) when I do something, I do it well. Its reliability alpha coefficient is 0.78. Higher scores indicate a greater sense of positive self-esteem.

The emotional distress measure (derived from the CAC) was developed by the National Longitudinal Survey of Children and Youth (NLSCY) (Statistics Canada, 1995) utilizing the emotional disorder/ anxiety scale derived from the Ontario Child Health Study (Boyle, Offord, Racine, Fleming, Szatmari, & Sanford, 1993). It consists of eight questionnaire items: a) appearing unhappy, sad, or depressed; b) crying a great deal; c) being too fearful or nervous; d) being worried; e) not as happy as other children; f) appearing miserable, tearful, or distressed; g) being high-strung or tense; and h) having trouble enjoying him/herself. Each item has three response categories: 0.never or not true, 1.sometimes or somewhat true, and 2.often or very true. The reliability coefficient for this scale is 0.79. Higher scores represent higher levels of emotional distress.

Independent Variables

Four independent variables of social isolation in relation to peers are included as predictors: perceived peer rejection based on ethnic background, feelings of disconnectedness from others at school, perceived relationships with peers, and the absence of close friendships.

Perceived peer rejection based on ethnic background (derived from CAC) was assessed by utilizing the scale of peer discrimination/ peer victimization experiences. It includes two types of peer rejection forms: first, *direct* forms of hostile behaviours (hitting, name-calling, pushing, being insulted in front of people, threatening) and second, *indirect* forms of hostile behaviours (ignoring, excluding in social interaction). This scale contains the four following items: a) by other students *at school* in *direct* forms of hostile behaviours; b) by other students *at school* in *indirect* forms of hostile behaviours; c) by other students *outside school* in *direct* forms of hostile behaviours; and d) by other students *outside school* in *indirect* forms of hostile behaviours. For youth respondents, to facilitate understanding of peer rejection experiences based on ethnic background, the questions were preceded by the following introduction: "People sometimes get treated unfairly because of who they are - I mean because they look different, were born outside of Canada, speak with an accent, or because of the color of their skin. I want you to think about the last month and tell me whether you were treated unfairly because of who you are". Each item has two-response choices: 0.no and 1.yes. The "yes" responses were summed in order to arrive at a final peer rejection score (from 0 to 4).

The feelings of disconnectedness from others (derived from the CAC) were measured by a single question about the experiences of psychological isolation or exclusion at school: the child feels like an outsider or left out of things at school. It has a five-point Likert scale, ranging from 0.never to 4.all the time. All responses were recoded into two categories: 0.no-feelings of disconnectedness from others (never or rarely) and 1.yes- feelings of disconnectedness from others (some of the time, most of the time or all the time).

Perceived relationships with peers (derived from the CAC) were assessed by utilizing the social acceptance and close peer relationship scale which was derived from two sources, the Peer Relationships Subscale (Marsh, 1988) and the study by Beiser et al. (1993). It consists of four statements: a) I have a lot of friends; b) I get along easily with others my age; c) others my age want me to be their friend and; d) most others my age like me. Each item has five response categories from 0.strongly disagree to 4.strongly agree. Its reliability coefficient is 0.74. Higher scores represent higher levels of positive peer relationships.

The absence of close friendships (derived from the CAC) was measured with a single questionnaire item: how often do you share your secret and private feeling with your close friends? It has a five-point Likert scale: 0.all the time, 1.most of the time, 2.some of the time, 3.rarely, and 4.never. The response categories were transformed into a dichotomous variable, coded as either 0.the presence of close friendship (all the time, most of the time, or some of the time) and 1.the absence of close friendship (rarely or never).

Demographic and Background Variables

Demographic and background variables included four characteristics: child sex (male or female), parent education, low income family (poverty), ethnic group. Parent education (less than bachelor's degree or bachelor's degree/ higher), was constructed as a dichotomized variable. Family poverty was measured by the Low Income Cut-offs (LICO) of Statistics Canada based on total household income during the 12 months prior to the interview. Canada has no official poverty measure and the LICO is a relative measure based on family size and community size (Lightman, 2003). For the purpose of this study (focusing on family poverty), families with a total income below 75% of the LICO were classified as living in poverty. A household income above 75% of the LICO was coded as *above poverty line*, and a household income below 75% of the LICO was coded as *below the poverty* line. To retain cases with income missing data and to avoid uncertain assumptions of imputed data, another category for *income not reported* was created. Among the three categories, *above poverty line* was used as the reference group in regression models.

Ethnic group is considered as a proxy measure in the current study as it is the marker that differentiates one group from the other group in terms of their history, social and cultural heritage. To control for ethnic heterogeneity, four dummy variables were included in the regression models: Hong Kong, Philippines, Haiti, and Lebanon. Among five ethnic groups, Mainland Chinese group was used as the reference category because it represents the largest group of immigrants in Canada (Statistics Canada, 2008).

Data Analysis

A range of descriptive analyses was first performed to describe the sample and characteristics. Comparative analyses (ANOVA, followed by Turkey post hoc comparisons) were conducted to determine whether there were significant differences among ethnic groups on any of the variables included in the current study. To examine the effects of social isolation factors, a series of multiple regression models were tested for each of two dependent variables. The self-esteem and emotional distress scales were regressed on perceived peer rejection based on ethnic background, feelings of disconnectedness from others, perceived relationships with peers, and the absence of close friendships, controlling for demographic and background variables.

RESULTS

Descriptive statistics for demographic and background characteristics are presented in Table 1. The sample consisted of 44.0% males and 56.0% females. The results indicated that 42.5% of PMK (mostly the mother) had a bachelor's degree. Based on the family income, 49.0% of the immigrant families lived in poverty. The percentages of ethnic origin were 25.5% for Mainland China, 18.7% for Hong Kong, 17.4% for the Philippines, 18.5% for Haiti, and 19.8% for Lebanon.

Table 1. Descriptive Statistics of Study Variables

	Mean or Percentage	S.D.	Observed Range
Background variables			
Child sex (female)	56.0%		
PMK education (bachelor's degree)	42.7%		
Low income family (poverty)	49.0%		
Ethnic group			
Mainland Chinese	25.5%		
Hong Kong Chinese	18.7%		
Filipino	17.4%		
Haitian	18.5%		
Lebanese	19.8%		
Independent variables			
Perceived peer rejection	0.77	1.20	0 – 4
Feelings of disconnectedness	16.2 %		
Perceived peer relationships	12.27	2.48	0 – 16
Absence of close friendships	28.7%		
Dependent variables			
Self-esteem	8.42	2.54	0 – 12
Emotional distress	4.72	3.21	0 – 16

Table 2 shows mean scores and proportions for each of the study variables to identify major differences in social isolation and psychological outcome variables across the ethnic groups. Statistically significant differences were found for five variables: feelings of disconnectedness from others, perceived peer relationships, absence of close friendships, self-esteem, and emotional distress. In terms of feelings of disconnectedness from others at school, Hong Kong and Mainland Chinese adolescents reported the higher scores on this scale, followed by Filipino, Lebanese, and Haitian groups. Post-hoc analyses indicated that Haitian and Lebanese adolescents were significantly higher in scores for the perception of positive peer relationships than other Asian groups (Mainland Chinese, Hong Kong, and Filipino). As for the absence of close friendships, Lebanese and Haitian adolescents reported the lower rates on this measure, followed by Hong Kong, Filipino, and Mainland Chinese groups. The difference of self-esteem across ethnic groups was marginally significant (p = .065), although this did not reach the .05 level of statistical significance. Hong Kong adolescents scored the lowest on this scale among all ethnic groups. The analyses revealed that the mean scores for emotional distress were significantly different across the ethnic groups, indicating that Hong Kong and Filipino adolescents reported higher levels of emotional distress than did other groups.

Table 2. Study Variables by Ethnic Group

Variables	Mean or Percentage					Statistical Test (X^2 or F)	P-Value
	M. Chinese	H.K.	Filipino	Haitian	Lebanese		
Independent variables							
Perceived peer rejection	0.75	0.82	0.95	0.65	0.68	F=0.79	P= .531
Feelings of disconnectedness	21.4%	23.5%	16.2%	8.20%	9.9%	X^2=12.33	p < .05
Perceived peer relationships	11.44[a]	11.22[a]	11.88[a]	13.47[b]	13.53[b]	F=21.87	p < .001
Absence of close friendships	40.2%	28.2%	31.2%	25.9%	14.4%	X^2=17.07	p < .01
Dependent variables							
Self-esteem	8.46	7.76	8.75	8.35	8.77	F=2.23	p = .065
Emotional distress	3.96 [a]	5.89[b]	5.04[ab]	4.57[a]	4.49[a]	F=4.90	p < .001

Note: Means with different superscripts (‘a’ and ‘b’) differed significantly (p < .05) across ethnic groups according to the results of Turkey post-hoc analyses, with a = lowest mean value.

*p < .05, **p < .01, ***p < .001 (two-tailed X^2 tests)

Multiple regression analyses were performed to examine each relationship among demographic background variables, social isolation variables, and psychological outcomes. Table 3 shows the associations of demographic background variables, perceived peer rejection based on ethnic background, feelings of disconnectedness from others, perceived relationships with peers, and the absence of close friendships with adolescents’ self-esteem and emotional distress.

For the self-esteem scale, the independent variables accounted for 10.1 percent of the variance (adjusted R^2=0.101, R^2=0.125). The results showed the significant effects of demographic variables, perceived peer rejection based on ethnic background, feelings of disconnectedness from others, and perceived relationships with peers on the self-esteem scale. Among the demographic background variables, the ethnic group effect was significant, indicating that Hong Kong and Haitian adolescents reported lower levels of self-esteem than did those from Mainland China group. Perceived peer rejection based on ethnic background and feelings of disconnectedness from others were negatively related to self-esteem. Perceived relationships with peers were found to contribute positively to greater self-esteem, while the effect of the absence of close friendships was not significant.

Table 3. Regressions of Self-esteem and Emotional Distress on Social Isolation Variables - Background Variables, Perceived Peer Rejection, Feelings of Disconnectedness, Perceived Peer Relationships, and the Absence of Close Friendships

	Self-esteem			Emotional Distress		
	B	β	S.E	B	β	S.E
Background variables						
Child sex (female)	-.288	-.056	.234	.696	.108	.297
PMK education	-.168	-.033	.283	-.036	-.005	.359
Low income family (poverty)	-.287	-.056	.250	-.214	-.033	.315
Hong Kong	**-.813***	-.124	.398	**1.858*****	.224	.502
Philippines	-.021	-.003	.368	**1.093***	.126	.464
Haiti	**-.927***	-.142	.421	1.016	.124	.530
Lebanon	-.477	-.075	.381	**1.055***	.133	.530
Independent variables						
Perceived peer rejection	**-.222***	-.106	.099	**.439*****	.166	.124
Feelings of disconnectedness	**-.703***	-.103	.329	**1.324****	.153	.415
Perceived peer relationships	**.260*****	.255	.053	**-.181****	-.140	.066
Absence of close friendships	-.116	-.021	.264	.227	.032	.332
Constant	**6.324*****		.740	**5.169*****		.931
R^2	.125			.156		
Adjusted R^2	.101			.132		

Note: Significant differences appear in boldface.
$*p < .05$ $**p < .01$ $***p < .001$

The second regression model for emotional distress accounted for 13.2 percent of the variance (adjusted R^2=0.132, R^2=0.156). The results indicated statistically significant relationships between demographic variables, perceived peer rejection based on ethnic background, feelings of disconnectedness from others, perceived relationships with peers, and emotional distress. Among ethnic groups, Hong Kong, Filipino and Lebanese adolescents reported higher levels of emotional distress, compared to Mainland Chinese adolescents. Perceived peer rejection based on ethnic background and feelings of disconnectedness from others were positively associated with emotional distress. Perceived relationships with peers made a significant contribution to emotional distress, revealing that adolescents having better relationships with peers were more likely to show lower levels of emotional distress. However, the significant effect of the absence of close friendships was not observed in the regression model.

DISCUSSION AND CONCLUSION

This chapter has been guided by the research questions pertaining to the potential social isolation factors of immigrant youth and their impact on psychological adjustment, using a study sample of five visible minority populations. The results indicate that the experiences of social isolation in relation to peers are associated with self-esteem and emotional distress of immigrant youth in early adolescence.

The results suggest that perceived peer rejection based on ethnic background can constitute a critical factor of social isolation for immigrant youth negatively affecting their outcomes. The data showed that perceived peer rejection based on ethnic background was related to displaying decreased self-esteem and increased emotional distress. This link between peer rejection and negative outcomes is supported by previous research on immigrant children (Graham, 2006; Oxman-Martinez et al., 2012), indicating that negative peer experiences might result in impairing the development of friendships and decreasing self-esteem. As revealed by our study, a sense of psychologically being isolated at school can be a critical factor of social isolation in understanding psychological adjustment of immigrant youth. The results showed that feelings of disconnectedness from others at school are associated with low self-esteem and high emotional distress. For immigrant youth, a sense of acceptance or inclusion by peers within the school community is a crucial part of their successful adaptation process

(Suarez-Orozco, Suarez-Orozco, Todorova, 2008). However, their unique characteristics such as differences in cultural norms on social behaviours, language barriers, and discrimination may provide additional challenges to form their potential friendships, compared to native-born youth.

Our findings also showed that perceived relationships with peers was a significant predictor of psychological adjustment among immigrant youth. The results indicated that perceived peer relationships were related to high levels of self-esteem and contributed to low levels of emotional distress. Affective bonds that immigrant youth establish in their peer groups can be one of the critical factors in coping with psychological distress in a new host society. This finding is consistent with previous research (Gibson, Gandara & Koyama, 2004; Way & Phal, 2001), indicating that positive peer interactions are related to emotional well-being. Surprisingly, our data demonstrated that no significant effect of the absence of close friendships was found, while perceived peer relationships *in general* was consistently associated with psychological outcomes. In this study, the quality of peer relationships was measured by sharing secret and private feelings with close friends. It seems that immigrant youth in our sample, due to their age, may not have fully developed close, intimate friendships to the degree where effects are experienced with regard to psychological outcomes. As well, during the early adolescence as a transitional period, meaningful peer relations are not only important, but also parent support is still vital to help early adolescents overcome adjustment difficulties (Collins, 1990). It may be possible that the effect of forging close friendships appears saliently later in adolescence. Further longitudinal research of the New Canadian Children and Youth (NCCYS) will allow better understanding of this issue.

When analyzing variations of the social isolation factors and psychological outcomes across the ethnic groups, we found significant contrast among the groups. On the one hand, immigrant youth from the Mainland Chinese group in our sample showed the lack of close friendships, but they reported low levels of emotional distresses. This finding suggests that despite the presence of risk factors contributing to social isolation, Mainland Chinese immigrant youth demonstrated better psychological outcomes and resilience. It seems that these immigrant youth who lack close relationships with friends could potentially find protective influence through positive relationships with significant others such as their parents. Research on Chinese Canadian families (Tian, 1999) indicates that one of the most distinguishing characteristics of immigrant families is the strong relationship between parents and children which may serve as a protective factor for immigrant youth's adjustment stresses. However, on the other hand, immigrant youth from the Hong Kong group showed unfavourable relational status including higher levels of feelings of disconnectedness from others and low levels of positive peer relationships. Hong Kong immigrant youth also reported adverse outcomes including lower levels of self-esteem and higher levels of emotional distress. These findings suggest that overall, Hong Kong immigrant youth are at a higher risk for poor social relationships and psychological adjustment difficulties than those from other ethnic groups in our sample. The differences in the prevalence of social isolation contributing psychological outcomes across diverse ethnic groups, provide stepping stones toward more detailed investigation of factors that may affect immigrant youth's adjustment within and across cultures. Further research is also needed to explore the protective factors that help to produce resilience and positive outcomes for those immigrant youth who live under negative circumstances.

Another significant difference in the experiences of social isolation was found among ethnic groups. Compared to immigrant youth with Asian backgrounds (Mainland Chinese, Hong Kong, and Filipino groups), those from Haitian and Lebanese groups showed more positive outcomes in terms of social isolation factors. They reported lower levels of feelings of disconnectedness and the absence of close friendships as well as higher levels of positive peer relationships. These findings may be related to official language proficiency, French being the Quebec official language. Given the fact that Haiti and Lebanon have had in the past some French colonial links, it seems that Asian ethnic immigrant youth are more likely to have language-related adjustment difficulties, in spite of compulsory French immersion classes. Language barriers may prevent them from effectively communicating and showing their strengths. The study on language competence and peer relationships among immigrant children (Von Grunigen, Kochenderfer-Ladd, Perren, & Alsaker; 2012) indicates that children's ability to communicate effectively with peers is related to their language ability as well as their social behaviour such as their interactions with peers that either promote or hinder the development of healthy peer relationships. With respect to the results of social isolation factors, it may be that Asian immigrant youth are at higher risk due to language barriers, language-dependent social skills and cultural norms such as initiating pro-social interactions and setting limits or boundaries with peers.

Although this study provides empirically important findings in understanding the experiences of social isolation among immigrant youth and their impact on psychological outcomes, there are some study limitations that need to be addressed. While the study includes a relatively large sample size of immigrant youth in early adolescence, there is an inherent limitation in sampling hard to reach subpopulations without a probability sampling method. Second, sample groups were recruited from the region of Greater Montreal in the province of Quebec where the social and educational systems are different from other Canadian provinces. Thus the findings must be interpreted with caution to the wider Canadian context and may not be generalized to immigrant youth in other parts of Canada. Lastly, since the study results are based on cross-sectional data, the direction of causal relationships between study variables cannot be determined. Future longitudinal analyses of the New Canadian Children and Youth Study are necessary to disentangle the direction of variable effects, and help identify the processes of influence of various environmental contexts on immigrant adolescents' adjustment and developmental outcomes over time.

In closing, this study demonstrates the significant role that peer relations play in the psychological adjustment of immigrant youth in early adolescence. Ethnic-based peer rejection, a sense of psychological isolation at school, perceived peer relationships emerge as critical effects that influence self-esteem and emotional distress of immigrant youth. These findings highlight the need to consider unique factors related to migration and ethnicity within the social relational context. After migration, immigrant youth need to re-establish their social relationships and support networks along with the adaptation process on a daily basis, whereas native-born youth in a host society often form and maintain stable social relationships. Thus understanding the roles of these significant factors is vital as immigrant youth encounter obstacles to adapt to a new society. Research knowledge will enable the development of more effective policies and programs aimed at helping immigrating youth cope with their unique challenges. Finally, it is hoped that results of the current chapter on social isolation and psychological adjustments among early adolescent immigrants offer further impetus to lessen social isolation and promote more inclusive processes of immigrant youth.

ACKNOWLEDGMENTS

This paper is a product of the New Canadian Children and Youth Study (Principal Investigators: Morton Beiser, Robert Armstrong, Linda Ogilvie, Jacqueline Oxman-Martinez, Joanna Anneke Rummens), a national longitudinal survey of the health and well-being of more than 4,000 immigrant and refugee children living in Montreal, Toronto, Winnipeg, Edmonton, Calgary and Vancouver. The NCCYS is a joint collaboration between university researchers affiliated with Canada's four Metropolis Centres of Excellence for research on immigration and settlement, and community organizations representing Afghani, Hong Kong Chinese, Mainland Chinese, Latin American (Salvadorian, Guatemalan, Colombian), Ethiopian, Haitian, Iranian, Kurdish, Lebanese, Filipino, Punjabi, Serbian, Somali, Jamaican, Sri Lankan Tamil, and Vietnamese immigrants in Canada. The NCCYS team is comprised of: investigators from eight universities representing multiple disciplines and involving faculty and trainees at various levels; research associates; immigrant/refugee community advisors representing sixteen immigrant communities; plus a research staff comprised of post-doctoral trainees, national coordinators, site coordinators, research assistants and numerous interviewers at each site. Major funding for the project has been provided by the Canadian Institutes of Health Research (CIHR grants FRN-43927 and PRG-80146), Canadian Heritage, Citizenship and Immigration Canada (CIC), Health Canada, Justice Canada, Alberta Heritage Foundation for Medical Research, Alberta Learning, B.C. Ministry of Social Development and Economic Security, B.C. Ministry of Multiculturalism and Immigration, Fonds de Recherche du Québec: Société et Culture (FRQ-SC), Manitoba Labour and Immigration, OASIS (CIC), and the Ontario, Prairies and Quebec Metropolis Centres of Excellence for research on immigration and settlement.

References

Alvarez, A. N., Juang, L., & Liang, C. T. (2006). Asian American and racism: When bad things happen to "model minorities". *Cultural Diversity and Ethnic Minority Psychology*, 12, 477-492.

Asher, S. R., & Paquette, J. A. (2003). Loneliness and peer relations in childhood. *Directions in Psychological Science, 12*, 75-78.

Beiser, M., Hamilton, H., Rummens, J. A., Oxman-Martinez, J., Ogilvie, L., Humphrey, C., & Armstrong, R. (2010). Predictors of emotional problems and physical aggression among children of Hong Kong Chinese, Mainland Chinese and Filipino immigrants to Canada. *Social Psychiatry and Psychiatric Epidemiology, 45*, 1011-1021.

Beiser, M., Lancee, W., Gotowiec, A., Sack, W., & Redshirt, R. (1993). Measuring self-perceived role competence among First Nations and non native children. *Canadian Journal of Psychiatry, 38,* 412-419.

Boivin, M., Hymel, S.,&Bukowski,W.M. (1995). The roles of social withdrawal, peer rejection, and victimization by peers in predicting loneliness and depressed mood in children. *Development and Psychopathology*, *7*, 765 - 786.

Boyle, M. H., Offord, D. R., Racine, Y., Fleming, J. E., Szatmari, P., & Sanford, M. (1993). Evaluation of the revised Ontario Child Health Study scales. *Journal of Child Psychological Psychiatry. 34*, 189-213.

Broderick, P. C., & Blewitt, P. (2006). *The life span: human development for helping professionals*. Upper Saddle River, NJ: Pearson Education, Inc.

Chen, X., He, Y., Oliveira, A.M. D., Coco, A. L., Zappulla, C., Kaspar, V., et al. (2004). Loneliness and social adaptation in Brazilian, Canadian, Chinese and Italian children: A multi-national comparative study. *Journal of Child Psychology and Psychiatry and Allied Disciplines*, *45*(8), 1373-1384.

Citizenship and Immigration Canada. (2006). *Facts and figures: Immigration overview: Permanent residents*. Retrieved from http://abacus.library.ubc.ca/handle/10573/42569?mode=full&submit_simple=Show+full+item +record.

Collins, W. A. (1990). Parent-child relationships in the transition to adolescence: Continuity and change in interaction, affect, and cognition. In R. Montemayor, G. R. Adams, & T. P. Gullotta (Eds.). *From childhood to adolescence: A transitional period?* (pp. 85-106). Beverly Hills, CA: Sage Publications.

Cooper, S.M., McLoyd, V., Wood, D., & Hardaway, C. (2008). The mental health consequences of racial discrimination for African American adolescents. In S. Quintana & C. McKown (Eds.), Handbook of race, racism and the developing child (pp. 278-312). Hoboken, NJ: Wiley.

Fisher, C. B., Wallace, S. A., & Fenton, R. E. (2000). Discrimination distress during adolescence. *Journal of Youth and Adolescence*, 29, 679-695.

Fox, N. A., Henderson, H. A., Marshall, P. J., Nichols, K. E., & Ghera, M. M. (2005). Behavioral inhibition: Linking biology and behavior within a developmental framework. *Annual Review in Psychology*, 56, 235-262.

Fuligni, A. J. (2004). The adaptation and acculturation of children from immigrant families. In U. P. Gielen, & J. Roopnarine, (Eds.). *Childhood and adolesc*ence (pp. 297-318). Westport, Conn.: Praeger.

Garcia-Coll, C., & Szalacha, L. A. (2004). The multiple contexts of middle childhood. *Future of Children, 41*(2), 81-97.

Gibson, M., Gandara, P., & Koyama, J. P. (2004). *School connections: U.S. Mexican youth, peers, and school adjustment*. New York: Teacher's College Press.

Graham, S. (2006). Peer victimization in school: Exploring the ethnic context. *Current Directions in Psychological Science, 15(6),* 317-321.

Greene, M. L., Way, N., & Phal, K. (2006). Trajectories of perceived adult and peer discrimination among Black, Latino, and Asian American adolescents: Patterns and psychological correlates. *Developmental Psychology*, 42, 218-238.

Grossman, J. M., & Liang, B. (2008). Discrimination distress among Chinese American adolescents. *Journal of Youth and Adolescence*, 3, 1-11.

Hall-Lande, J. A., Eisenberg, M. E., Christenson, S. L., & Neumark-Sztainer, D. (2007). Social isolation, psychological health, and protective factors in adolescence. *Adolescence*, 42(166), 265-286.

Hay, D. F., Payne, A., & Chadwick, A. (2004). Peer relations in childhood. *Journal of Child Psychology & Psychiatry*, *45*, 84–108.

Hartup, W. W., & Stevens, N. (1997). Friendships and adaptation in the life course. *Psychological Bulletin, 121*, 355 – 370.

Hymel, S., Vaillancourt, T., McDougall, P., & Renshaw, P. D. (2002). Peer acceptance and rejection in childhood. In P. K. Smith & C. H. Hart (Eds.), *Blackwell handbook of childhood social development* (pp. 265–284). Oxford: Blackwell Publishing.

Juvonen, J., & Graham, S. (2001). *Peer Harassment in school: The plight of the vulnerable and the victimized.* New York, NY: Guilford.

Ladd,G.W. (2006). Peer rejection, aggressive orwithdrawn behavior, and psychological maladjustment from age 5 to 12: An examination of four predictive models. *Child Development*, 77, 822-846.

Laursen, B., Bukowski, W., Aunola, K., & Nurmi, J. (2007). Friendship moderates prospective associations between social isolation and adjustment problems in young children. *Child Development,* 78(4), 1395-1404.

Levitt, M. J., Guacci-Franco, N., & Levitt, J. L. (1994). Social support and achievement in childhood and early adolescence: a multicultural study. *Journal of Applied Developmental Psychology*, 15, 207-222.

Lightman, Ernie. 2003. *Social policy in Canada.* Don Mills, ON: Oxford University Press.

Marsh, H. W. (1988). S*elf-description Questionnaire, SDQ manual: the psychologicalcCorporation.* New York, NY: Harcourt Brace & Company.

Ngo, H. V. & Schleifer, B. (2005, spring). Immigrant children and youth in focus. Canadian Issues, 29-33.

Ontario Council of Agencies Serving Immigrants (OCASI). (2009). *Newcomer youth settlement guide for service providers.* Toronto, ON: Ontario Council of Agencies Serving Immigrants.

Omidvar, R., & Richmond, T. (2003). *Immigrant Settlement and Social Inclusion in Canada.* Toronto, ON: The Laidlaw Foundation.

Oxman-Martinez. J., Rummens, A. J., Moreau, J., Choi, Y. R., Beiser, M., Ogilvie, L., & Armstrong, R. (2012). Perceived ethnic discrimination and social exclusion: Newcomer immigrant children in Canada. *American Journal of Orthopsychiatry, 82(3),* 376-388.

Qualter, P., Brown, S.L., Munn, P., & Rotenberg, K.J. (2010). Childhood loneliness as a predictor of adolescent depressive symptoms: An 8-year longitudinal study. *European Child and Adolescent Psychiatry*, *19(6)*, 493-501.

Rhodes, J. E. (2002). *Stand by me: The risks and rewards of youth mentoring relationships.* Cambridge: Haravard University Press.

Rubin, K.H. & Burgess, K. (2001). Social withdrawal. In M.W. Vasey & M.R. Dadds (Eds.), *The developmental psychopathology of anxiety.* (pp. 407-434). Oxford, UK: Oxford University.

Rubin, K. H., Coplan, R. J., & Bowker, J. C. (2009). Social withdrawal in childhood. *Annual Review of Psychology*, 60, 1–31.

Rubin, K. H., Chen, X., McDougall, P., Bowker, A., & McKinnon, J. (1995). The Waterloo longitudinal project: Predicting internalizing and externalizing problems in adolescence. *Development and Psychopathology*, 7, 751-764.

Rubin, K. H., Fredstrom, B., & Bowker, J. (2008). Future directions in. . . Friendship in childhood and early adolescence. *Social Development*, *17*(4), 1085-1096.

Suarez-Orozco, C., Suarez-Orozco, M., & Todorova, I. (2008). *Learning a new land: Immigration students in American society.* Cambridge, MA: Harvard University Press.

Statistics Canada. (1995). *National longitudinal survey of children: Overview and survey instruments for 1994-1995; data collection cycle 1.* Ottawa, ON: Ministry of Industry.

Statistics Canada. 2008. "*2006 Census data products. Ethnic origin, 2006 counts for Canada.*" Cata. no.97-562-XWE2006002. Ottawa, ON: Statistics Canada.

Tian, G. (1999). *Chinese-Canadian, Canadian-Chinese: Coping and adapting in North America.* Queenston, ON: The Edwin Mellen Press.

Verkuyten, M., Kinket, B., & Wielen, C. V. (1997). Preadolescents' understanding of ethnic discrimination. *The Journal of Genetic Psychology,* 158(1), 97–112.

Von Grunigen, R., Kochenderfer-Ladd, B., Perren, S., & Alsaker, F. D. (2012). Links between local language competence and peer relations among Swiss and immigrant children: the mediating role of social behavior. *Journal of School Psychology,* 50(2), 195-213.

Waldrip, A. M., Malcolm, K. T., & Jensen-Campbell, L. A. (2008). With a little help from your friends: The importance of high-quality friendships on early adolescent adjustment. *Social Development, 17*(4), 832–852.

Way, N. (2006). The cultural practice of close friendships among urban adolescents in the United States. In X. Chen, D. French, and B. Schneider (Eds.), *Peer relations in cultural context* (pp.403-425). New York: Cambridge university Press.

Way, N., & Phal, K. (2001). The predictors of friendship quality among ethnic minority, low-income adolescents. *Journal of Research on Adolescence, 11,* 325-349.

Wigfield, A., Eccles, J. S., Maclver, D., et al. (1991). Transitions during early adolescence: Changes in children's domain-specific self-perceptions and general self-esteem across the transition to junior high school. *Developmental Psychology*, 27, 552-565.

Wiles, J., Bondi, J., & Wiles, M. T. (2006). *The essential middle school.* Upper Saddle River, NJ: Pearson Education, Inc.

Woods, S., Done, J., & Kalsi, H. (2009). Peer victimisation and internalising difficulties: The moderating role of friendship quality. *Journal of Adolescence*, *32*(2), 293–308.

Zhou, Z., Perverly, S., Xin, T., Huang, A. S., & Wang, W. (2003). School adjustment of first-generation Chinese American adolescents. *Psychology in the Schools*, 40, 71-84.

In: Social Isolation, Participation ...
Editor: Kristin T. Rowe

ISBN: 978-1-63482-505-4

Chapter 3

LONELINESS, INHIBITION, AND FRIENDLESSNESS: ASSOCIATIONS WITH ADOLESCENTS' APPEARANCE-RELATED CONCERNS, ATTRACTIVENESS, AND TEASING ABOUT APPEARANCE

Haley J. Webb*[*]*, Samantha Ferguson and Melanie J. Zimmer-Gembeck
Griffith University, School of Applied Psychology and Griffith Health Institute, Behavioural Basis of Health, Gold Coast, Queensland, Australia

ABSTRACT

The aim of the present study was to identify which aspects relating to appearance-related concerns and social experiences, and status amongst peers, are relevant to understanding social isolation in early adolescents. In a sample 387 boys and girls (M_{age} = 12.0 years, 44.4% males), we assessed both objective and subjective indicators of social isolation. Specifically, social isolation was measured based on adolescents' self-reported loneliness, inhibition in social contexts, and social acceptance. We also used nominations of friendship to identify youth who had no

[*] Corresponding author: Dr Haley Webb, School of Applied Psychology, Behavioural Basis of Health, Griffith University, Gold Coast Australia. 4222. E-mail: haley.webb@griffithuni.edu.au, Phone: +61 (0)7 5678 8688.

reciprocated friends (total friendlessness) or whose closest friend was not reciprocated (close friendlessness). As predicted, adolescents who felt socially isolated (i.e., inhibited, lonely, or low social acceptance), reported more dissatisfaction with their body and concerns about peer rejection because of the way they look, as well as elevated appearance teasing by peers and by family members. These youth were also less accepted by their peers. Notably, adolescents who felt inhibited, lonely, or less socially accepted were not more likely to be friendless. Finally, adolescents were at increased odds of both total and close friendlessness when they were less accepted by their peers, while the odds of close friendlessness were higher among adolescents who reported higher body dissatisfaction and, surprisingly, lower among those who reported more appearance teasing from family members. The results of this study have implications for supporting socially isolated and vulnerable youth, and highlight the need for continued research to examine the longitudinal associations of social isolation with appearance-related concerns and social adversity.

Classic and contemporary theories, based on evolutionary, social, and developmental perspectives, argue that humans are motivated from the very earliest days of life to seek, establish and maintain social interactions and close relationships with others (Ainsworth, 1989; Baumeister & Leary, 1995; Fromm-Reichmann, 1959). According to this belongingness hypothesis, these desires are innate given their evolutionary benefit, and they are some of the most profound of all human motivations (Baumeister & Leary, 1995; Deci & Ryan, 1985; Maslow, 1943). This need to belong, and to be related and connected to close others, is often first focused on caregivers (Bowlby, 1969). Subsequently, establishing and maintaining meaningful relationships with others of about the same age, including belonging to peer groups and forming close friendships, becomes increasingly important. Such relationships with peers are thought to facilitate children's burgeoning trust in others within and outside the family, enhance a sense of security, and promote a positive sense of self competence and esteem (Erickson, 1963; Harter, 1999; Zimmer-Gembeck, 2001).

When this need to belong outside the family of origin is unfulfilled, *actual* social isolation in the form of friendlessness can be the culprit. Also, however, *perceived* social isolation in the form of loneliness may occur despite the existence of friends and close relationships with others. For example, research has shown that some adolescents feel lonely (i.e., they report a feeling of lack of belongingness or a feeling of not being connected to others) regardless of reporting many friends (Asher & Paquette, 2003), and some adolescents show no signs of distress despite their peers reporting that they are highly disliked by most others (Ferguson & Zimmer-Gembeck, 2014; Zimmer-Gembeck, Hunter, & Pronk, 2007). Thus, for some youth, objective friendlessness may be the best indicator of social isolation, but this may or may not give rise to subjective feelings of loneliness or social isolation. Finally, there are a select group of young people whose social inhibition may partially explain why they are objectively more socially isolated and why they report more loneliness and other forms of distress (Rubin, Coplan, & Bowker, 2009). This makes it imperative to assess social isolation using measures that are objective indicators of social connection, as well as assessing subjective feelings of social isolation from others.

When examining the social correlates and antecedents of objective indicators and perceived social isolation among children and adolescents, it is not surprising that one common thread is exposure to rejection, often by classmates or other peers (Bruch & Cheek, 1995; Ladd & Troop-Gordon, 2003; London, Downey, Bonica, & Paltin, 2007; Parker & Asher, 1993; Rowe, Zimmer-Gembeck, Nesdale, & Rudolph, in press). Not only are rejected children often able to readily describe painful experiences of separation and exclusion by peers and/or family members, there is also the possibility that early rejection experiences can facilitate an inability to cope with future social interactions (Butler, Doherty, & Potter, 2007; Margalit, 2010).

Appearance as Linked with Rejection and Social Isolation

Body Image and Appearance Concerns

Body image and appearance concerns are among the top three issues concerning Australian youth (along with coping with stress, and school or study problems; Ivancic, Fildes, Perry, & Christensen, 2014). Teasing and rejection are often more frequent for children who are perceived to be different from others (Sweeting & West, 2001), and this difference can come in the form of appearance that diverges from the norm or ideal societal standards (Webb & Zimmer-Gembeck, 2014). For example, children who are less attractive as judged by their peers are often lower in popularity (Borch, Hyde, & Cillessen, 2011; Wang, Houshyar, & Prinstein, 2006) and children who are overweight or obese are more likely to experience peer victimization and bullying (Griffiths, Wolke, Page, & Harwood, 2006). In fact, previous research has shown that body dissatisfaction and teasing about appearance are prominent correlates of low self-esteem, and social and emotional adjustment problems among youth (Eisenberg et al., 2006; Harter, 2002; Paxton, Neumark-Sztainer, Hannan, & Eisenberg, 2006; Webb & Zimmer-Gembeck, 2014).

To summarize, research suggests that social isolation, including actual isolation and perceived loneliness, reflects unmet needs for interpersonal intimacy and belongingness, and can have ongoing adverse social effects. Studies have shown that elements relating to physical appearance may be important for understanding why some children feel rejected or experience victimization by peers, yet to our knowledge, no previous study has examined adolescents' appearance-related concerns and experiences, or adolescents' social status amongst their peers, to determine which aspects are most relevant to understanding when adolescents are more socially isolated. Accordingly, the aim of the present study was to examine the role of a number of appearance-related attributes, concerns, and experiences in understanding or predicting social isolation in young adolescents. Specifically, sensitivity to appearance-based rejection (appearance-RS), body dissatisfaction, appearance-related teasing by peers and family members, and peer-reported ratings of attractiveness, social acceptance, and popularity were examined as correlates of social isolation. To ensure a comprehensive assessment of social isolation, both objective and subjective indicators were utilized, including adolescents' perceived loneliness, inhibition in social contexts, acceptance by peers, as well as friendlessness status (i.e., unreciprocated friendship nominations).

Appearance-Related Rejection Sensitivity

Exposure to rejection has been linked to the development of the social-cognitive processing bias referred to as rejection sensitivity (RS), which describes the tendency to anxiously expect, readily perceive, and overreact to rejection (Downey, Bonica, & Rincon, 1999; Downey, Feldman, Khuri, & Friedman, 1994; Feldman & Downey, 1994; Ferguson & Zimmer-Gembeck, 2014). The RS model (Downey et al., 1994), derived in part from Bowlby's (1969) attachment theory, views sensitivity to rejection as an extension of internalised early parent and peer rejection experiences (Downey, et al., 1999). According to Bowlby, children develop 'internal working models' through connections with a primary caregiver and, later, via associations with others including peers. The RS model also draws from social cognitive theory (Downey et al., 1999), relying in particular on attribution theory to propose that early parent and peer rejection experiences affect current and future social information processing through attributions for others' behaviours, and the formation and subsequent activation of relational schemas.

These working models serve to filter perceptions of social situations, expectations and memories. Thus, infant attachment style is likely to have some impact on the way in which people approach new social situations and social encounters later in life, and these new social encounters continue to affect individuals' working models of relationships (Bowlby, 1963; Raikes & Thompson, 2006). In this model, early rejection by parents and/or peers is expected to sensitize children to expect rejection in the form of two accompanying affective responses, anxiety or anger. Although all individuals are likely to have negative emotional reactions when rejection is actually experienced, these responses are expected to be inflated among individuals high in RS compared to others, and this is expected to occur in social situations where rejection is possible or implied (Zimmer-Gembeck & Nesdale, 2014). Thus, this rejection-sensitive processing bias has negative implications for mental health and has been found to influence the course of interactions in ways that confirm and maintain rejection expectations (Downey, Freitas, Michaelis, & Khouri, 1998; Croft & Zimmer-Gembeck, 2014).

With the application of the RS model to particular research pursuits, some studies have chosen to focus on personal-rejection sensitivity (personal-RS; Downey & Feldman, 1996), whereby general anxious expectations of rejection are not linked to a specific attribute. More recently, however, other researchers have focused on the tendency to develop specific RS biases (e.g., Mendoza-Denton, Downey, Purdie, Davis, & Pietrzak, 2002; Park, 2007), including those that are appearance-based (Bowker, Thomas, Spencer, & Park, 2013; Webb, Zimmer-Gembeck, & Donovan, 2014; Webb & Zimmer-Gembeck, 2014). Specifically, appearance-based rejection sensitivity (appearance-RS) is the tendency to anxiously expect, readily perceive, and overreact to signs of rejection *based on personal appearance* (Park, 2007). Appearance-RS has been linked to a number of maladaptive outcomes, including poor self-esteem, social withdrawal, social anxiety, and a sense of self-worth as dependent on appearance (Bowker, et al., 2013; Park, 2007; Park & Pinkus, 2009). High appearance-RS individuals also show elevated symptoms of body dysmorphic disorder and more endorsement of cosmetic surgery (Calogero, Park, Rahemtulla, &Williams, 2010; Park, Calogero, Young, & DiRaddo, 2010).

The study of appearance-RS is particularly important among early adolescents, because this developmental period is fraught with concerns about peer-perceived physical attractiveness amidst the bodily changes characteristic of pubertal growth (Bowker et al., 2013; Ricciardelli & McCabe, 2001). In this connection, Lieberman and colleagues (2001) found that early adolescents anticipated greater popularity and more peer acceptance based on their perceived level of physical attractiveness. Furthermore, negative bodily perceptions in this age group may manifest as emotional distress (Barker & Bornstein, 2010; Williams & Currie, 2000). Despite this importance, there is a paucity of research on appearance-RS among children and adolescents, with only three published studies focused on adolescence (Bowker, et al., 2013; Webb et al., 2014; Webb & Zimmer-Gembeck, 2014). Therefore, more attention is needed to address this important area of research in order to isolate the factors that may be linked with early onset of heightened appearance-RS.

SOCIAL ISOLATION: FRIENDLESSNESS, LONELINESS, AND SOCIAL INHIBITION

Subtle yet important distinctions have emerged in the literature when conceptualizing social isolation (see Zavalata, Samuel, & Mills, 2014 for a review). For example, Laursen and colleagues (2007) consider social isolation as an extension of peer-initiated exclusion, whereas Cacioppo and Hawkley (2003) considered only the subjective elements of social isolation in the form of loneliness. Furthermore, Fine and Spencer (2009) proposed two distinct characteristics; social and affective isolation, including low levels of social interaction *as well as* feelings of loneliness (Findlay & Cartwright 2002). That is, the quality and quantity of social interactions were considered important in order to maintain definitional integrity. Hortulanus and colleagues (2006) proposed a multidimensional typology, which takes into account both of these important elements, as well as an additional layer of social inhibition. This typology comprises the socially competent, the socially inhibited, the lonely, and the socially isolated. Taken together, in the present study, social isolation is conceptualized as the absence of social relationships (friendlessness), the perceived absence of certain types of social relationships (loneliness) and a lack of contact with others via social withdrawal (social inhibition).

Friendlessness

For early adolescents (typically considered to range from 10 to 14 years of age), friendships may be particularly important, as this is a time of life when the structure and the quality of peer relationships produce both new demands and new opportunities for social and emotional growth. Therefore, when reciprocal dyadic relationships elude early adolescents, critical opportunities for social skill development may be thwarted. In his classic theory, Sullivan (1953) described how, beginning in preadolescence (around 8 years of age) and continuing throughout early adolescence, friends can enable social comparisons, satisfy needs for acceptance, and empower the practice of co-operation, compromise, and competition. Friendships also provide opportunities to complete important early adolescent developmental tasks, including individuation, enhancing autonomy, and renegotiating relationships (Bagwell & Schmidt, 2011). For example, perceived general self-worth in adulthood has been uniquely related to reports of mutual friendship in early adolescence (Bagwell, Newcomb, & Bukowski, 1998).

Erath and colleagues (2010) found that having close friendships moderated the relation between social anxiety and psychosocial maladjustment (e.g., low self-efficacy). In other work, children without friends (compared to those with friends) have reported more depression and other forms of psychological maladaptation, including disruptiveness, low academic performance, and low prosocial behaviour (Ladd, 1990; Parker & Asher, 1993; Parker, Rubin, Price, & de Rosier, 1995). Laursen and colleagues (2007) also found that having friends (as opposed to being friendless) reduced the relation between internalizing and externalizing behaviour in Grade 2. Furthermore, among rejected and victimized children within the peer group there is also often a distinct lack of reciprocal friendships (Ladd & Troop-Gordon, 2003; Parker & Asher, 1993).

Loneliness

As well as objective friendlessness, the experience of social isolation can also be highly subjective, with loneliness arising from a perceived discrepancy between ideal and actual interpersonal relationships (Qualter, Brown, Munn, & Rotenberg, 2010). To feel lonely has been described as a sad or aching sense of isolation, associated with a longing for contact or closeness with others (Asher & Paquette, 2003; Parkhurst & Hopmeyer, 1999). Loneliness in childhood has demonstrated stability over time and has been associated with later maladjustment (i.e., depression, anxiety, anger, suicide, alcoholism, poor self-concept, psychosomatic problems; Al-Yagon, 2008; Heinrich & Gullone, 2006). In contemporary research studies, it has been argued that loneliness in itself is a crucial marker of social relationship deficits. Generally, children report loneliness as comprising distressed emotions and prolonged solitude (Margalit, 2010). The pervasive emotional and cognitive experience of loneliness has also been found to be strongly associated with rejection experiences within the peer group in middle childhood and early adolescence (London et al., 2007).

Social Inhibition

In the present study, the term *social inhibition* is utilized, which is most akin to Rubin's (1982) classic description of (passive) social withdrawal, which describes a process of self-selected isolation from one's peers stemming from factors internal to the child or early adolescent. This may begin early in life as a tendency towards shyness in social situations, as well as sensitivity and hypervigilance to one's environment (Coplan, Girardi, Findlay, & Frohlick, 2007; Kagan, 2001; Kagan, Reznick, & Snidman, 1988). These stable behavioural patterns often persist over time, placing an early adolescent at risk of social anxiety, which can present as a fear of negative appraisal as well as distress and avoidance of social situations (Coplan, et al., 2007; La Greca & Stone, 1993). Through the promotion of social solitude, these manifestations of social anxiety can inhibit friendship formation and foster feelings of loneliness. In this way, we suggest that social inhibition may be one mechanism through which actual and perceived social isolation may manifest during this developmental period. With the magnification of social pressures inherent in the early adolescent age group, consequences of displaying a tendency towards social inhibition can persist across the lifespan (Hirshfeld et al., 1992; Pine, Helfinstein, Bar-Haim, Nelson, & Fox, 2008). In particular, responses to these behavioural patterns may range from peer rejection to further isolation to bullying, because social inhibition deviates substantially from peer group norms (Bruch & Cheek, 1995).

THE CURRENT STUDY

In sum, a sense of belonging is often attributed to successful appearance-related experiences, and achieving social status within the peer group. Research has shown that these elements are strongly associated with adolescents' social and emotional adjustment problems (i.e., self-esteem, depression, and anxiety; Eisenberg, Neumark-Sztainer, Haines, & Wall, 2006; Harter, 2002; Paxton et al., 2006). The aim of the present study was to extend this previous research to the examination of appearance-related concerns in conjunction with social status amongst peers. This was done to elucidate which aspects of personal appearance and social status are relevant to understanding socially isolated adolescents. In the present study, we include both objective and subjective indicators of adolescents' social isolation. Specifically, social isolation was measured based on early adolescents' self-reported loneliness, inhibition in social contexts, and how much they perceived themselves to be accepted (i.e., liked) by their classmates. We also used nominations of friendship to identify youth who had no reciprocated close friends (i.e., no one they nominated as a friend nominated them back) or whose closest friend was not reciprocated.

We examined the associations of these five measures of social isolation with early adolescents' sensitivity to appearance-based rejection (appearance-RS), body dissatisfaction, appearance-related teasing by peers and family members, and peer-reported ratings of attractiveness, acceptance, and popularity. We anticipated that similarities and differences in the correlations of different measures of social isolation would reveal how some measures identify youth demonstrating different struggles with body concerns and different experiences of problems with peers or within their families. We also expected, however, that the findings would reveal the prominent role of heightened body and appearance concerns, and teasing about appearance, in social isolation, regardless of how it was measured.

METHOD

Participants

Participants were 387 students (172 males, 215 females) from three independent schools in an urban area of Australia. Participants were 9 years 8 months to 14 years old (M_{age} = 12.0 years, *SD* = 10.8 months), and were predominantly white/Caucasian (78.6%), or Asian (15.2%). The overall response rate was 42.4%, with 15.7% of parents actively declined participation, and the remainder did not return a consent form.

Procedure

Study approval was obtained from the Griffith University Human Research Ethics Committee. Active parental consent was required to participate. Consent forms were sent home with children, and to encourage the return of consent forms to classroom teachers, a cupcake party was awarded to the class within each grade, at each school, that returned the most consent forms, regardless of whether parents consented to their child participating. A small gift was also given to participating students when the survey was completed. The questionnaire, which comprised additional measures not included in this paper, was completed by participants in their regular classrooms, taking approximately 60 minutes.

Utilizing a planned missing design to reduce the burden on participants (Little, Jorgensen, Lang, & Moore, 2014), two dependent variables and two independent variables in this study (social inhibition, loneliness, body dissatisfaction, and appearance teasing by family members) were administered to only 50% of the sample. To retain all participants in all analyses, multiple imputation was used to replace these planned missing values, and pooled results from multiple imputation are reported.

Measures

Social isolation

Social isolation was measured in five ways. First, the 6-item social inhibition subscale of the Social Anxiety Scale for Children – Revised (La Greca & Stone, 1993) was used to assess adolescents' social inhibition. An example item is: "I feel shy even with peers I know very well." Participants indicated on a 5-point scale how much they felt each statement was true for them (1 = *not true*, 5 = *very true*). Averaging all items formed the total score, and Cronbach's α was .72.

Second and third, we created measures of total friendlessness and close friendlessness. From a provided list of all students in the same grade, participants specified the ID codes of their friends. Total friendlessness was defined as no reciprocated friendship nominations. Close friendlessness was defined as an unreciprocated closest friend nomination. For both friendlessness variables, participants with reciprocated friendships coded as 0, and participants with unreciprocated friendship nominations coded as 1. Where friendship reciprocity could not be verified, due to all of a participant's nominated friends or a participant's closest friend not participating in the study, friendlessness was imputed.

Fourth, we measured perceived loneliness. This was measured with a single item from the Short Mood and Feelings Questionnaire - Child (Angold et al., 1995); "I felt lonely". Participants were asked to consider how true the statement was for them over the last two weeks (1 = *not true*, 5 = *very true*).

Fifth, self-reported liking was assessed using a single item, which evaluated the degree to which each participant perceived that he or she was liked by his or her classmates ("How much do you feel that other kids in your school like you?"; 1 = *not at all*, 5 = *very much*). This measure is referred to as *self-reported peer acceptance*.

Appearance-RS

The Adolescent Appearance-RS Scale (Webb et al., 2014) was modified from the Appearance-RS Scale (Park, 2007) to be appropriate for use for adolescents. Participants were asked to imagine themselves in 10 hypothetical scenarios (e.g., "Your boyfriend/girlfriend of 3 months is considering breaking up with you"), and indicate on a 6-point scale their anxiety/concern about being rejected based on their appearance (e.g., "How concerned or anxious would you be that he/she wants to break up with you because of the way you look?"; 1 = *not concerned*, 6 = *very concerned*), and their expectation of appearance-related rejection in the imagined scenario (e.g., "Do you think your boyfriend/girlfriend is considering breaking up with you because of the way you look?"; 1 = *No!!*, 6 = *Yes!!*). Anxious concern was multiplied by expectation of rejection for each item, and these 10 product scores were averaged to form the total score. A higher score indicated greater appearance-RS. Cronbach's α was .92.

Body Dissatisfaction

The 22-item Body-Image Ideals Questionnaire (BIQ; Cash, 2000) was used to assess body dissatisfaction. Participants were asked to rate how closely they resemble their physical ideal (0 = *exactly as I am*, 3 = *very unlike me*), in relation to a variety of attributes (e.g., skin complexion, facial features, weight, muscle tone, definition and strength). Participants then indicated how important they felt it was to embody that ideal (0 = *not important*, 3 = *very important*). As per the BIQ manual, discrepancy scores of 0 were recoded as -1, then the discrepancy was multiplied by importance score for each item, and these product scores were averaged to form the total score. The total score has a possible range of -3 (very important and congruent actual-ideal) to 9 (very important and maximum actual-ideal discrepancy). Cronbach's α was .84.

Teasing about appeArance

Derived from the Weight Teasing Subscale of the Perceptions of Teasing Scale (POTS; Thompson, Cattarin, Fowler, & Fisher, 1995), three items assessed perceived appearance teasing by peers, and two items assessed appearance teasing by family members. For example: "Do people your age / your sisters or brothers / your parent or parents make fun of you because of your weight or looks?" Participants rated the frequency of teasing (1 = *never*, 5 = *very often*), as well as their degree of distress (1 = *not upset*, 5 = *very upset*). The average of the product of the teasing frequency and teasing distress items formed the appearance teasing by peers (Cronbach's α = .79) and appearance teasing from family (Cronbach's α = .81) subscales.

BMI

Trained researchers measured participant height and weight, to enable the calculation of BMI (weight kg/height m^2).

Peer Acceptance

To measure participants' acceptance by peers, classmates rated how much they liked each other classmate ("Please indicate how much you like each of your classmates"; 1 = *not at all*, 6 = *very much*). These items were averaged to form a peer-reported acceptance score for each participant.

Attractiveness and Popularity

To assess attractiveness and popularity of participants, a list of all students in the same grade was provided. Each participant nominated up to 10 classmates who he or she perceived to be "the most good-looking" and, on a separate item, who he or she perceived to be "the most popular." Nominations received for each participating student were summed and standardized within grade to adjust for unequal class sizes. Because attractiveness and popularity were highly correlated, $r = .84$ for boys and .74 for girls, these two scores were averaged to create a measure referred to as *social prominence*.

RESULTS

Descriptive Statistics and Correlations between Measures

Mean and SDs of all measures, and correlations between all variables are presented in Table 1. Regarding associations between measures of social isolation, adolescents' who were more socially inhibited were also lonelier, whereas adolescents who felt more accepted by their peers were less lonely and inhibited. Total and close friendlessness were positively correlated, but were not associated with inhibition, loneliness or self-reported acceptance.

Measures of social isolation were also associated with higher appearance-related concerns and poorer peer relationship experiences. All self-report measures of social isolation (loneliness, inhibition, and low peer acceptance) were correlated to greater appearance concerns and more appearance teasing by peers and family members, and with peer reports of lower acceptance and social prominence. Loneliness and self-reported acceptance, but not inhibition, were associated with peer-reported acceptance, with lonelier adolescents, and those who felt less accepted, were reported by their peers to be less accepted. Adolescents who were friendless were also reported by their peers to be less accepted, but only close friendlessness (not total friendlessness) was associated with greater body dissatisfaction and lower peer-reported social prominence.

Unique Associations of Appearance-Related Concerns and Relationships with Social Isolation

Table 2 presents the results of three multiple regression analyses, which were used to test the unique correlates of self-reported social isolation (social inhibition, loneliness, and self-reported peer acceptance). In the first model, social inhibition was regressed on BMI and all measures of appearance-related concerns and social relationships. In the second and third models, loneliness and self-reported peer acceptance were regressed on all measures.

Table 1. Correlations between all Measures ($N = 387$)

	Measures	1	2	3	4	5	6	7	8	9	10	11	12
1	Social Inhibition	-											
2	Loneliness	.22**	-										
3	SR peer acceptance	-.21**	-.28**	-									
4	Total friendlessness[a]	-.07	.01	-.01	-								
5	Close friendlessness[a]	.03	-.01	-.06	.50**	-							
6	BMI	.12*	.11*	-.05	.07	.04	-						
7	Body dissatisfaction	.42**	.37**	-.29**	.01	.12*	.44**	-					
8	Appearance-RS	.40**	.43**	-.22**	-.02	-.01	.22**	.55**	-				
9	Teasing - peers	.26**	.36**	-.24**	.04	-.01	.21**	.41**	.47**	-			
10	Teasing - family	.36**	.26**	-.13*	-.07	-.08	.22**	.46**	.54**	.40**	-		
11	PR acceptance	-.06	-.14*	.19**	-.17**	-.18**	-.04	-.05	.01	-.08	-.02	-	
12	Social prominence	-.12*	-.11*	.13*	-.08	-.11*	-.14*	-.13*	-.04	-.05	-.07	.28**	-
	Mean	2.30	2.01	3.46	-	-	18.44	0.95	10.60	5.77	4.86	3.23	-0.03
	SD	0.68	0.92	1.01	-	-	2.96	1.60	7.31	10.20	3.63	0.61	0.86

$p < .05$. ** $p < .01$.

SR = self-reported, PR = peer-reported.

[a]Reciprocated friends or closest friend = 0, unreciprocated friends or closest friend = 1.

Table 2. Results of Regressing Social Inhibition, Loneliness, and Self-reported Acceptance on All Measures (*N* = 387)

	β	*t*	*p*	β Lower 95% CI	β Upper 95% CI
Social Inhibition, F (7, 379) = 17.73, $p < .001$, $R^2 = .25$					
Independent variables					
BMI	-.09	-1.73	.08	-.04	.01
Body dissatisfaction**	.28	4.67	<.01	.07	.17
Appearance-RS**	.18	3.03	<.01	.01	.03
Appearance teasing - peers	.01	0.27	.79	-.01	.01
Appearance teasing - family*	.14	2.55	.01	.01	.05
Peer-reported acceptance	-.03	-0.63	.53	-.13	.07
Social prominence	-.07	-1.54	.12	-.13	.02
Loneliness F (7, 379) =18.02, $p < .001$, $R^2 = .25$					
Independent variables					
BMI	-.07	-1.46	.15	-.05	.01
Body dissatisfaction**	.18	2.96	<.01	.03	.17
Appearance-RS**	.28	4.62	<.01	.02	.05
Appearance teasing - peers**	.17	3.16	<.01	.01	.02
Appearance teasing - family	-.02	-0.41	.68	-.03	.02
Peer-reported acceptance*	-.11	-2.35	.02	-.30	-.03
Social prominence	-.05	-1.11	.27	-.15	.04
Self-Reported Peer Acceptance, F (7, 379) = 8.83, $p < .001$, $R^2 = .14$					
Independent variables					
BMI	.10	1.91	.06	-.01	.07
Body dissatisfaction**	-.25	-3.89	<.01	-.24	-.08
Appearance-RS	-.08	-1.18	.24	-.03	.01
Appearance teasing - peers*	-.13	-2.29	.02	-.02	-.01
Appearance teasing - family	.06	1.08	.28	-.02	.05
Peer-reported acceptance**	.15	3.01	<.01	.09	.41
Social prominence	.06	1.22	.22	-.04	.19

*$p < .05$. **$p < .01$.

Table 3. Results of Logistic Regression Model Predicting Friendlessness (N = 387)

	B	*SE*	Wald Statistic	*p*	OR Upper 95% CI	OR Lower 95% CI
Total Friendlessness, χ^2 (7, N = 387) = 17.39, p = .02, R^2 = .04						
Independent variables						
BMI	0.14	0.12	1.43	.23	0.92	1.44
Body dissatisfaction	0.07	0.28	0.07	.79	0.62	1.88
Appearance-RS	-0.01	0.06	0.02	.88	0.87	1.12
Appearance teasing - peers	0.01	0.03	0.18	.67	0.95	1.08
Appearance teasing - family	-0.25	0.15	2.72	.10	0.58	1.05
Peer-reported acceptance*	-1.43	0.62	5.39	.02	0.07	0.80
Social prominence	-0.92	1.09	0.72	.40	0.05	3.35
Close Friendlessness, χ^2 (7, N = 387) = 28.84, p < .001, R^2 = .07						
Independent variables						
BMI	-0.01	0.07	0.01	.95	0.87	1.14
Body dissatisfaction**	0.48	0.16	9.36	<.01	1.19	2.19
Appearance-RS	-0.02	0.04	0.28	.60	0.92	1.05
Appearance teasing - peers	-0.01	0.02	0.36	.55	0.94	1.03
Appearance teasing - family*	-0.18	0.07	6.70	.01	0.73	0.96
Peer-reported acceptance**	-0.91	0.32	8.31	<.01	0.22	0.75
Social prominence	-0.45	0.36	1.50	.22	0.31	1.31

*p < .05. **p < .01.

Note. B = Unstandardized Coefficient, SE = Standard Error, OR = Odds Ratio. R^2= Cox & Snell.

Reciprocated friends or closest friend = 0, unreciprocated friends or closest friend = 1.

The independent variables explained significant variance in social inhibition (F [7, 379] = 17.73, p < .001, R^2 = .25), loneliness (F [7, 379] = 18.02, p < .001, R^2 = .25), and self-reported acceptance (F [7, 379] = 8.83, p < .001, R^2 = .14) (see Table 2). There were unique associations of social inhibition with body dissatisfaction, appearance-RS, and appearance teasing by family members. Adolescents who were more socially inhibited were more dissatisfied with their bodies, were higher in appearance-related sensitivity to rejection, and felt more teased by their family about their appearance. For loneliness, there were unique associations with body dissatisfaction, appearance-RS, appearance teasing by peers, and peer-reported acceptance. Adolescents who were lonelier were more dissatisfied with their bodies, were higher in sensitivity to appearance-related rejection, felt more teased by their peers about their appearance, and were less liked by their peers at school. For perceived acceptance by peers, this had unique associations with body dissatisfaction, appearance teasing by peers, and peer-reported acceptance. Adolescents who perceived themselves to be less accepted by their peers were more dissatisfied with their bodies, felt more teased by their peers about their appearance, and were rated by their peers as less liked.

Unique Associations of Appearance-Related Concerns and Relationships with Friendlessness

Logistic regression was used evaluate whether friendless participants could be discriminated from non-friendless participants based on their appearance-related concerns and peer status (see Table 3). Two models were estimated, with the first predicting total friendlessness and the second predicting close friendlessness. In the first model, peer-reported acceptance was the only significant predictor of total friendlessness, with the odds of being friendless lower for youth who were more liked by their peers (OR = .24, p = .02). Close friendlessness was predicted by peer acceptance (OR = .40, p = .004), body dissatisfaction (OR = 1.61, p = .002), and teasing by family (OR = .83, p = .01). Adolescents had an increased odds of having no reciprocated close friend if they reported greater body dissatisfaction, and their odds of close friendlessness was decreased if they were more accepted by their peers and, surprisingly, if they were more teased by their family about their appearance.

DISCUSSION

We investigated whether appearance-related concerns and social adversity, and social status were associated with social isolation in early adolescents. More specifically, we considered how similarities and differences in the correlations of self-reported loneliness, inhibition in social contexts, peer acceptance, and friendlessness would identify youth who struggle with appearance concerns and experience adversity in their peer and family relationships. We expected that each of these elements of social isolation would highlight the prominent role of heightened body and appearance concerns, and teasing about appearance, in social isolation for early adolescents.

Perceived Social Isolation, Appearance Concerns and Social Adversity

Overall, the present study found that the three indicators of perceived social isolation, namely social inhibition, loneliness, and low peer acceptance, were associated with higher appearance-related concerns and poorer relationship experiences within the peer and family context. Consistent with expectations, adolescents who reported more inhibition or loneliness, or less peer acceptance, were more likely to report dissatisfaction with their physical appearance and concerns about being rejected by peers because of the way they look, as well as reporting elevated teasing experiences by peers and by family members. In addition, adolescents who felt socially inhibited, lonely, or less socially accepted were less accepted by their peers, and were rated as less socially prominent. Multivariate models revealed that heightened appearance concerns and appearance teasing by family members were most important in understanding social inhibition, while heightened appearance concerns and appearance teasing by peers, and lower peer acceptance, stood out as unique predictors of loneliness and self-reported social acceptance. Concerns about physical appearance become a key issue during adolescence, due to the physical changes during puberty and emerging interest in romantic and sexual relationships (Miller & Benson, 1999; Stice, 2003). When we consider the comorbidities of body dissatisfaction and distress about appearance-based rejection, such as low self esteem, interpersonal withdrawal, and social evaluative concerns (Bowker, et al., 2013; Cash, Theriault, & Annis, 2004), it is not surprising that appearance concerns are also linked with perceptions of social isolation.

It is notable that adolescents who felt inhibited, lonely, or less socially accepted were not more likely to be friendless. This finding is consistent with prior research which shows that some adolescents feel lonely regardless of the presence of friendship connections (Asher & Paquette, 2003), and that some adolescents are socially inhibited within mutual friendships, but that these relationships tend to lack positive friendship qualities, such as intimacy, pleasure, and helpfulness (see Parker, Rubin, Erath, Wojslawowicz, & Buskirk, 2006).

Friendlessness, Appearance Concerns and Social Adversity

Friendlessness in this study was measured in two ways; total friendlessness included participants for whom all friendship nominations were unreciprocated, and close friendlessness included participants whose closest friend nomination was unreciprocated. Using multivariate logistic regression, it was found that adolescents were at increased odds of both forms of friendlessness when they were less accepted by their peers, while the odds of close friendlessness were also higher among adolescents who reported higher body dissatisfaction. It is notable that while total and close friendlessness were moderately correlated (r = .50), close friendless adolescents were not all totally friendless. Research suggests that mutual friendships during childhood are protective of psychological adjustment and provide a context for learning important interpersonal skills (Erdley, Nangle, Newman, & Carpenter, 2001; Newcomb & Bagwell, 1995). As such, the benefits conferred by mutual friendships elude totally friendless youth. The results of the present study suggest that totally friendless adolescents are less accepted by their peers, but are not differentiated from their non-friendless peers on any other measured variable. In contrast, adolescents who did not have a mutual best friend could be distinguished by heightened appearance concerns, and lower peer acceptance. Our results are consistent with previous research that showed friendless children were less accepted by peers (Kingery & Erdley, 2007). Unlike in the present study, friendlessness was positively associated with loneliness; however the association did not remain in multivariate analyses. Given that the models proposed in the present study explained at least double the variance in self-reported social isolation measures compared to the friendlessness measures, appearance concerns and experiences reflect a portion of the picture in trying to understand the individual and social characteristics of friendless adolescents, and highlight the importance of examining other individual and social characteristics of these socially isolated youth (e.g., deficient prosocial skills, disruptiveness; Bowker, Fredstrom, Rubin, Rose-Krasnor, Booth-LaForce, & Laursen, 2010; Vitaro, Brendgen, & Wanner, 2005).

Finally, it should be noted that, once all other measures were accounted for in a multiple logistic regression model, being teased by family members was associated with *lower* odds of having an unreciprocated closest friend, rather than the converse association that was expected. It is possible that when families tease adolescents about their weight, teens move away from the family and focus their energies on forging and maintaining very close relationships with their peers, making it more likely that their friendships would be reciprocated. Given that this association was not significant when we examined simple correlations, however, this finding could also be a statistical artefact due to a model suppression effect (e.g., teasing by family and body dissatisfaction were moderately correlated and suppression might be occurring because of this correlation).

Limitations and Future Directions

The key limitations of this study include the measurement of loneliness and self-reported social acceptance using single items, and the cross sectional design. The use of single item assessments may have restricted the scope of the measurement of social isolation (about which we attempted to compensate by using a multi-method approach), while the use of a cross sectional design prevents conclusions about the direction of effects. Elucidating the longitudinal associations of social isolation with individual and social concerns is an important avenue for future research, in order to identify the degree to which appearance concerns and adverse social experiences contribute to increasing social isolation over time, whether social isolation predicts the onset and worsening of appearance concerns and perceptions of adversity, or a combination of both. Longitudinal research would also be valuable in identifying mediators of these associations, as well as how these associations change throughout adolescence (i.e., increase, decrease, or are stable).

Conclusion

The findings provide support for our expectations regarding the significance of body image and concerns about appearance-based rejection, and appearance-related victimization experiences for socially isolated youth. Results revealed that adolescents who feel socially isolated tend to be more dissatisfied with their body, are more anxious about being rejected by their peers because of their appearance, report more appearance teasing from peers or family members, and are less socially accepted. However, many of these youth retain mutual friendship connections. On the other hand, there are socially isolated youth who have no reciprocated friends or no reciprocated closest friend and experience low social acceptance by their peers. Nevertheless, although they may be somewhat more dissatisfied with their appearance, they are not more likely to feel inhibited, lonely, or socially disliked or to perceive greater teasing by their peers about their appearance.

REFERENCES

Ainsworth, M. S. (1989). Attachments beyond infancy. *American Psychologist*, *44*, 709-716. doi:10.1037/0003-066X.44.4.709

Al-Yagon, M. (2008). Maternal personal resources and children's socioemotional and behavioral adjustment. *Child Psychiatry and Human Development*, *39*, 283-298. doi:10.1007/s10578-007-0088-z

Angold, A., Costello, E. J., Messer, S. C., Pickles, A., Winder, F. & Silver, D. (1995). The development of a short questionnaire for use in epidemiological studies of depression in children and adolescents. *International Journal of Methods in Psychiatric Research*, 5, 237 - 249.

Asher, S. R. & Paquette, J. A. (2003). Loneliness and peer relations in childhood. *Current Directions in Psychological Science*, *12*, 75-78. http://dx.doi.org/ 10.1111/1467-8721.01233

Bagwell, C. L., Newcomb, A. F. & Bukowski, W. M. (1998). Preadolescent friendship and peer rejection as predictors of adult adjustment. *Child Development*, *69*, 140-153. doi:10.1111/j.1467-8624.1998.tb06139.x

Bagwell, C. L. & Schmidt, M. E. (2011). The friendship quality of overtly and relationally victimized children. *Merrill-Palmer Quarterly*, *57*, 158-185. doi:10.1353/mpq.2011.0009

Barker, E. T. & Bornstein, M. (2009). Global self-esteem, appearance satisfaction, and self-reported dieting in early adolescence. *The Journal of Early Adolescence*, *30*, 205-224. doi:10.1177/0272431609332936

Baumeister, R. F. & Leary, M. R. (1995). The need to belong: desire for interpersonal attachments as a fundamental human motivation. *Psychological Bulletin*, *117*, 497-529. doi:10.1037/0033-2909.117.3.497

Borch, C., Hyde, A. & Cillesen, A. H. N. (2011). The role of attractiveness and aggression in high school popularity. *Social Psychology of Education*, *14*, 23–39. doi:10.1007/ s11218-010-9131-1

Bowker, J. C., Fredstrom, B. K., Rubin, K. H., Rose-Krasnor, L., Booth-LaForce, C. & Laursen, B. (2010). *Journal of Social and Personal Relationships*, *27*, 707-725. doi:10.1177/0265407510373259

Bowker, J. C., Thomas, K. K., Spencer, S. V. & Park. L. E. (2013). Examining appearance-based rejection sensitivity during early adolescence. *Journal of Research on Adolescence*, *23*, 375–388. doi:10.1111/jora.12003

Bowlby, J. (1969). *Attachment and loss*, Vol. *1*. *Attachment*. New York, NY: Basic Books.

Brunch M. A. & Cheek, J. M. (1995) Developmental factors in childhood and adolescent shyness. In: Heimberg R. G, Liwbowitz M. R, Hope D. A, Schneier F. R, (Eds). *Social phobia: Diagnosis, assessment, and treatment*. (163–192) New York: Guilford.

Butler, J. C., Doherty, M. S. & Potter, R. M. (2007). Social antecedents and consequences of interpersonal rejection sensitivity. *Personality and Individual Differences*, *43*, 1376-1385. doi:10.1016/j.paid.2007.04.006

Cacioppo, J. T., Hawkley, L. C. & Berntson, G. G. (2003). The anatomy of loneliness. *Current Directions in Psychological Science*, *12*, 71-74. doi:10.1111/1467-8721.01232

Calogero, R. M., Pina, A., Park, L. E. & Rahemtulla, Z. (2010). Objectification theory predicts college women's attitudes toward cosmetic surgery. *Sex Roles*, *63*, 32-41. doi:10.1007/s11199-010-9759-5

Cash, T. F. (2002). Cognitive behavioral perspectives on body-image. In T. F,. Cash, & T. Pruzinsky (Eds). *Body image: Handbook of theory, research, and clinical practice* (38-46). New York: The Guilford Press.

Cash, T. F., Theriault, J. & Annis, N. M. (2004). Body image in an interpersonal context: Adult attachment, fear of intimacy, and social anxiety. *Journal of Social and Clinical Psychology*, *23*, 89-103. doi:10.1521/jscp.23.1.89.26987

Coplan, R. J., Girardi, A., Findlay, L. C. & Frohlick, S. L. (2007). Understanding solitude: Young children's attitudes and responses toward hypothetical socially withdrawn peers. *Social Development*, *16*, 390-409. doi:10.1111/j.1467-9507.2007.00390.x

Croft, C. & Zimmer-Gembeck, M. J. (2014). Friendship conflict, conflict responses, and instability: Unique links to anxious and angry forms of rejection sensitivity, *Journal of Early Adolescence*, *34*, 1094-1119. doi:10.1177/0272431613518972

Deci, E. L. & Ryan, R. M. (1985). The general causality orientations scale: Self-determination in personality. *Journal of Research in Personality*, *19*, 109-134. doi:10.1037/0033-2909.125.6.627

Erath, S. A., Flanagan, K. S., Bierman, K. L. & Tu, K. M. (2010). Friendships moderate psychosocial maladjustment in socially anxious early adolescents. *Journal of Applied Developmental Psychology*, *31*, 15-26. doi:10.1016/j.appdev.2009.05.005

Erickson, E. H. (1963). *Childhood and Society* (2nd ed.). New York: Norton

Downey, G., Bonica, C. & Rincon, C. (1999). Rejection sensitivity and adolescent romantic relationships. In W. Furman, B. Bradford Brown, & C. Feiring (Eds.), *The development of romantic relationships in adolescence* (148–174). New York: Cambridge University Press.

Downey, G. & Feldman, S. I. (1996). Implications of rejection sensitivity for intimate relationships. *Journal of Personality and Social Psychology*, *70*, 1327-1343. doi:10.1037/ 0022-3514.70.6.1327

Downey, G., Feldman, S., Khuri, J. & Friedman, S. (1994). Maltreatment and childhood depression. In *Handbook of depression in children and adolescents* (481-508). New York: Springer.

Downey, G., Freitas, A. L., Michaelis, B. & Khouri, H. (1998). The self-fulfilling prophecy in close relationships: rejection sensitivity and rejection by romantic partners. *Journal of Personality and Social Psychology*, *75*, 545-560. doi:10.1037/0022-3514.75.2.545

Eisenberg, M. E., Neumark-Sztainer, D., Haines, J. & Wall, M. (2006). Weight-teasing and emotional well-being in adolescents: Longitudinal findings from Project EAT. *Journal of Adolescent Health*, *38*, 675-683. doi:10.1016/j.jadohealth.2005.07.002

Erdley, C. A., Nangle, N., Newman, J. E. & Carpenter, E. M. (2001). Children's friendship experiences and psychological adjustment: Theory and research. *New Directions for Child and Adolescent Development*, *91*, 5-24. doi:10.1002/cd.3

Feldman, S. & Downey, G. (1994). Rejection sensitivity as a mediator of the impact of childhood exposure to family violence on adult attachment behavior. *Development and Psychopathology*, *6*, 231-247. doi:10.1017/ S0954579400005976

Ferguson, S. & Zimmer-Gembeck, M. J. (2014). Associations of parental and peer rejection with preadolescents' loneliness: Emotional sensitivities as mediators. *Journal of Relationships Research*, *5*, e9. doi:10.1017/ jrr.2014.9

Findlay, R. & Cartwright, C. (2002). Social Isolation & Older People: A Literature Review. Report for Seniors Interest Branch & Ministerial Advisory Council Older People. *Brisbane: Australasian Centre on Ageing.*

Fine, M. & Spencer, R. (2009). Social isolation: Development of an assessment tool for HACC services. Centre for Research on Social Inclusion, New South Wales Department of Disability, Ageing and Home Care.

Fromm-Reichmann, F. (1959). Loneliness. *Psychiatry: Journal for the Study of Interpersonal Processes*, *22*, 1-15.

Griffiths, L. J., Wolke, D., Page, A. S. & Horwood, J. P. (2006). Obesity and bullying: Different effects for boys and girls. *Archives of Disease in Childhood, 91*, 121–125. doi:10.1136/adc.2005.072314

Harter, S. (1999). *The construction of the self: A developmental perspective.* Guilford Press.

Harter, S. (2002). Authenticity. In C. R. Snyder & S. J. Lopez (Eds.), *Handbook of positive psychology* (382–394). New York: Oxford University Press.

Heinrich, L.M. & Gullone, E. (2006). The clinical significance of loneliness: A literature review. *Clinical Psychology Review*, *26*, 695–718. doi:10.1016/j.cpr.2006.04.002

Hirshfeld, D. R., Rosenbaum, J. F., Biederman, J., Bolduc, E. A., Faraone, S. V., Snidman, N., ... & Kagan, J. (1992). Stable behavioral inhibition and its association with anxiety disorder. *Journal of the American Academy of Child & Adolescent Psychiatry*, *31*, 103-111. doi:10.1097/00004583-199707000-00012

Hortulanus, R., Machielse, A. & Meeuwesen, L. (2006). *Social isolation in modern society*, (Vol. *10*). New York, NY: Routledge.

Ivancic, L., Perrens, B., Fildes, J., Perry, Y. & Christensen, H. (2014). *Youth mental health report*, *June 2014.* Mission Australia and Black Dog Institute.

Kingery, J. N. & Erdley, C. A (2007). Peer experiences as predictors of adjustment across the middle school transition. *Education and Treatment of Children*, *30*, 73-88.

La Greca, A. M. & Stone, W. L. (1993). Social Anxiety Scale for Children-Revised: Factor structure and concurrent validity. *Journal of Clinical Child Psychology*, *22*, 17-27. doi:10.1207/s15374424jccp2201_2

Ladd, G. W. (1990). Having friends, keeping friends, making friends, and being liked by peers in the classroom: Predictors of children's early school adjustment. *Child Development*, *61*, 1081-1100. doi:10.1111/j.1467-8624.1990.tb02843.x

Ladd, G. W. & Troop-Gordon, W. (2003). The role of chronic peer difficulties in the development of children's psychological adjustment problems. *Child Development*, *74*, 1344-1367. doi:10.1111/1467-8624.00611

Laursen, B., Bukowski, W. M., Aunola, K. & Nurmi, J. E. (2007). Friendship moderates prospective associations between social isolation and adjustment problems in young children. *Child Development*, *78*, 1395-1404. doi:10.1111/j.1467-8624.2007.01072.x

Little, T. D., Jorgensen, T. D., Lang, K. M. & Moore, E. W. G. (2014). On the joys of missing data. *Journal of Pediatric Psychology*, *39*, 151-162. doi:10.1093/jpepsy/jst048

London, B., Downey, G., Bonica, C. & Paltin, I. (2007). Social causes and consequences of rejection sensitivity. *Journal of Research on Adolescence*, *17*, 481-506. doi:10.1111/j.1532-7795.2007.00531.x

Margalit, M. (2010). *Lonely children and adolescents: Self-perceptions, social exclusion and hope*, New York: Springer.

Maslow, A. H. (1943). A theory of human motivation. *Psychological Review*, *50*, 370-396. doi:10.1037/h0054346

Mendoza-Denton, R., Downey, G., Purdie, V. J., Davis, A. & Pietrzak, J. (2002). Sensitivity to status-based rejection: implications for African American students' college experience. *Journal of Personality and Social Psychology*, *83*, 896-918. doi:10.1037/0022-3514.83.4.896

Miller, B. C. & Benson, B. (1999). Romantic and sexual relationship development during adolescence. In W. Furman, B. B. Brown, & C Feiring (Eds.), *The development of romantic relationships in adolescence*, (99-121). NY, USA: Cambridge University Press.

Newcomb, A. & Bagwell, C. (1995). Children's friendship relations: A meta-analytic review. *Psychological Bulletin*, *117*, 306–347

Park, L. E. (2007). Appearance-Based Rejection Sensitivity: Implications for Mental and Physical Health, Affect, and Motivation. *Personality and Social Psychology Bulletin*, *33*, 490-504. doi:10.1177/0146167206296301

Park, L. E., Calogero, R. M., Young, A. F. & Diraddo, A. M. (2010). Appearance-based rejection sensitivity predicts body dysmorphic disorder symptoms and cosmetic surgery acceptance. *Journal of Social and Clinical Psychology*, *29*, 489-509. .doi:10.1521/ jscp.2010.29.5.489

Park, L. E. & Pinkus, R. T. (2009). Interpersonal effects of appearance-based rejection sensitivity. *Journal of Research in Personality*, *43*, 602-612. doi:10.1016/j.jrp.2009.02.003

Parker, J. G. & Asher, S. R. (1993). Friendship and friendship quality in middle childhood: Links with peer group acceptance and feelings of loneliness and social dissatisfaction. *Developmental Psychology*, *29*, 611-621. doi:10.1037/0012-1649.29.4.611

Parker, J. G., Rubin, K. H., Erath, S. A., Wojslawowicz, J. C. & Buskirk, A. A. (2006). Peer relationships, child development, and adjustment: A developmental psychopathology perspective. In D. Cicchetti, & D. J. Cohen (Eds. Vol. 1), *Developmental psychopathology, Theory and method* (2nd ed.), (pp. 419-493). Hoboken, NJ: John Wiley & Sons Inc.

Parker, J. G., Rubin, K. H., Price, J. M. & DeRosier, M. E. (1995). Peer relationships, child development, and adjustment: A developmental psychopathology perspective. In D. Cicchetti & D. Cohen (Eds. Vol. 2), *Developmental psychopathology: Risk, disorder, and adaptation*, (96-161). New York: Wiley.

Parkhurst, J. T. & Hopmeyer, A. (1999). Developmental change in the sources of loneliness in childhood and adolescence: Constructing a theoretical model. In K.J. Rotenberg & S. Hymel (Eds.), *Loneliness in childhood and adolescence*, (56–79). New York: Cambridge University Press

Paxton, S. J., Neumark-Sztainer, D., Hannan, P. J. & Eisenberg, M. E. (2006). Body dissatisfaction prospectively predicts depressive mood and low self-esteem in adolescent girls and boys. *Journal of Clinical Child and Adolescent Psychology*, *35*, 539-549. doi:10.1207/s15374424jccp3504_5

Pine, D. S., Helfinstein, S. M., Bar-Haim, Y., Nelson, E. & Fox, N. A. (2008). Challenges in developing novel treatments for childhood disorders: lessons from research on anxiety. *Neuropsychopharmacology*, *34*, 213-228. doi:10.1038/npp.2008.113

Qualter, P., Brown, S. L., Rotenberg, K. J., Vanhalst, J., Harris, R. A., Goossens, L., ... & Munn, P. (2013). Trajectories of loneliness during childhood and adolescence: Predictors and health outcomes. *Journal of Adolescence*, *36*, 1283-1293. doi:10.1016/ j.adolescence.2013.01.005

Raikes, H. A. & Thompson, R. A. (2006). Family emotional climate, attachment security and young children's emotion knowledge in a high risk sample. *British Journal of Developmental Psychology*, *24*, 89-104. doi:10.1348/026151005X70427

Ricciardelli, L. A. & McCabe, M. P. (2001). Children's body image concerns and eating disturbance: A review of the literature. *Clinical Psychology Review*, *21*, 325-344. doi:10.1016/S0272-7358(99)00051-3

Rubin KH. 1982. Nonsocial play in preschoolers: necessarily evil? *Child Development*, *533*, 651-57. doi:10.2307/1129376

Rubin, K. H., Coplan, R. J. & Bowker, J. C. (2009). Social withdrawal in childhood. *Annual Review of Psychology*, *60*, 141-171. doi:10.1146/ annurev.psych.60.110707.163642

Stice, E. (2003). Puberty and body image. In C. Hayward (Ed.), *Gender differences in puberty* (61-76). Cambridge, UK: Cambridge University Press.

Sullivan H. S. (1953). *The interpersonal theory of psychiatry*. New York: Norton.

Sweeting, H. & West, P. (2001). Being different: correlates of the experience of teasing and bullying at age 11. *Research Papers in Education*, *16*, 225-246. doi: 10.1080/02671520110058679

Thompson, J. K., Cattarin, J., Fowler, B. & Fisher, E. (1995). The perception of teasing scale (POTS): A revision and extension of the physical appearance related teasing scale (PARTS). *Journal of Personality Assessment*, *65*, 146-157. doi:10.1207/s15327752 jpa 6501_11

Vitaro, F., Brendgen, M. & Wanner, B. (2005). Patterns of affiliation with delingquent friends during late childhood and early adolescence: correlates and consequences. *Social Development*, *14*, 82-108. doi:10.1111/j.1467-9507.2005.00292.

Wang, S. S., Houshyar, S. & Prinstein, M. J. (2006). Adolescent girls' and boys' weight-related health behaviors and cognitions: Associations with reputation- and preference-based peer status. *Health Psychology*, *25*, 658–663. doi:10.1037/0278-6133.25.5.658

Webb, H. & Zimmer-Gembeck, M. J. (2014). The role of friends and peers in adolescent body dissatisfaction: A review and critique of 15 years of research, *Journal of Research on Adolescence*. doi:10.1111/jora.1208.

Webb, H. J., Zimmer-Gembeck, M. J. & Donovan, C. L. (2014). The appearance culture between friends and adolescent appearance-based rejection sensitivity. *Journal of Adolescence*, *37*, 347-358. doi:10.1016/ j.adolescence.2014.02.008

Williams, J. M. & Currie, C. (2000). Self-esteem and physical development in early adolescence: pubertal timing and body image. *The Journal of Early Adolescence*, *20*, 129-149. doi:10.1177/0272431600020002002

Zavaleta, D., Samuel, K. & Mills, C. (2014). *Social isolation: A conceptual and measurement proposal* (Vol. 67, p. 3). OPHI Working Papers.

Zimmer-Gembeck, M. J. (2002). The development of romantic relationships and adaptations in the system of peer relationships. *Journal of Adolescent Health*, *31*, 216-225

Zimmer-Gembeck, M. J., Hunter, T. A. & Pronk, R. (2007). A model of behaviors, peer relations and depression: Perceived social acceptance as a mediator and the divergence of perceptions. *Journal of Social and Clinical Psychology*, *26*, 273-302. doi:10.1521/jscp.2007.26.3.273

Zimmer-Gembeck, M. J. & Nesdale, D. (2013). Anxious and angry rejection sensitivity, social withdrawal, and retribution in high and low ambiguous situations. *Journal of Personality*, *81*, 29-38. doi:10.1111/j.1467-6494.2012.00792.x

In: Social Isolation, Participation … ISBN: 978-1-63482-505-4
Editor: Kristin T. Rowe

Chapter 4

AT WHAT TIME AND FOR HOW LONG FOR THE SOCIAL NEED TO BE DEPRIVED ARE IMPORTANT FOR THE OUTCOME: INTERPRETATION OF THE EFFECTS OF ISOLATION REARING BY DEVELOPMENTAL TIMING AND PERSISTENCE IN RAT MODELS

***Yia-Ping Liu*[1,2*]**
[1]Department of Physiology and Biophysics,
National Defense Medical Center, Taipei, Taiwan, ROC
[2]Department of Psychiatry, Tri-Service General Hospital,
Taipei, Taiwan, ROC

ABSTRACT

For any species with a social nature, isolation from other conspecific members is an environmental deprivation of a basic need. The sequelae of social isolation are multifarious, and may relate clinically to physiological and psychological abnormalities. The epigenetic theory holds that an unsatisfactory resolution of a particular stage would reflect a failure

* Correspondence: Liu, Yia-Ping MD., PhD; Department of Physiology, National Defense Medical Center, No.161,Section 6,Min-Chuan East Road ,Taipei 114, Taiwan. Telephone: 886-2-87923100, ext 18614; Fax: 886-2-87923153; E-mail: yiaping@ms75.hinet.net.

afterwards, thus raises the existence of a hypothetically critical time window during early life in which a temporary isolation rearing (IR) after weanling determines principally for physical, cognitive or emotional performance in adulthood. However, evidence also revealed that a long term, ongoing and cumulative IR since the weanling caused different, and sometime opposite effects in neural substrates and networks. It is therefore that the timing and the length of time play different roles in the IR effects, as they represent distinctive neural mechanisms for the individual to copy with the deprivation of social need. Based on the current developmental theories, the present article reviews the related IR works to date with an attempt to interpret the effects of social isolation in terms of social need, behavioral inhibition, cumulative stress and mismatch hypothesis, dopaminergic activity, and particularly addresses the importance of both the timing and the persistence of social isolation.

For development, epigenetic theory holds that it occurs in a scheduled sequential with several clearly defined stages, in which each stage must be satisfactorily resolved. If the resolution of a given stage proves unsuccessful, all subsequent stages would reflect that failure in a form of physical, cognitive, or emotional maladjustment (Erikson, 1975). Within such a conceptual framework, early life experience appears to have enduring effects across the life journey (Kraemer, 1992), as some psychologists said, from cradle to grave (Chopik et al., 2013).

For humans, Piaget and Bowlby substantialized this concept by showing that some basic cognitive schemata are necessary for achieving the later "adult thought" (Inhelder and Piaget, 1958; Beilin and Harry, 1994) and ~~a~~ an emotional tone existed between developing child and others (for example, the caretaker) is epigenetically important, in which "attachment", the term that Bowlby used to describe the emotional tone, only occurs when there is a warm, intimate physical contact (Bowlby, 1969). For any individual, the need of this relationship not only operates during the infancy when feeding is compulsively necessary, but also is required following weaning since things like, for example, close sibling connection, peer group experience and playful interaction all provide essential substrates for socialization and mental development (Erikson, 1975; Vaillant and Mukamal, 2001). Nevertheless, there are still considerable debates regarding many aspects of early life influences for biological understanding, such as their controlling variables, the precise patterns of abnormality to which certain aspects of behavior or psychology are sensitive, and to what extent these effects interact with genetic or environmental factors (Paykel and Hollyman, 1984; Paykel and Cooper,

1992; Harris and Brown, 1996). As human literature has offered almost no insight into the rationale of how early life effects can be translated into enduring effects, animal models turn to be useful if interpreted with due caution, as the process of attachment occurs also in non-human primate, and some other animals, such as rodents.

Rat Model of Social Separation

Early life manipulation of rats has been employed in examining the role of social attachment by two basic paradigms, maternal deprivation (MD) and social isolation, the latter in turn divided into isolation housing [IH, social isolation after puberty, usually executed after 12 weeks of age, (Jones and Robbins, 1989] and isolation rearing (IR, social isolation since weaning, until death). The MD paradigm refers to a repeated removal of pups from the dam during the neonatal period, typically between 5 to 20 days of age. In the case of IR, the main idea is to raise weaning animals in a situation of social separation. Typically, IR rats are allowed to see, smell and hear other rats but not indulge in social contact with them. The isolation paradigm begins around 21-23 days of age (i.e., post-natal day, PND), which is the time for weaning from their dam. The protocol will continue for at least 8 weeks before any behavioral testing or neurochemical approach. The effects of IR have been studied extensively from various aspects, as summarized as the following.

Vegetative Effects

IR rats have been reported to eat more under the condition of free feeding (Morgan and Einon, 1975) and to defecate less in a novel environment (Gentsch et al., 1981). For body weight, IR rats have been generally to weight more (Morgan, 1973), though in some studies they had been found to weigh less (Hunziker et al., 1996).

Locomotor Activity

Perhaps the most consistent effect of isolation rearing is to increase their locomotor activity in response to a novel situation (for review, see Hall, 1998). In fact, it would be more appropriate to term this character as "hyperreactivity" as the locomotor hyperactivity is dependent on the novelty of the testing environment (Gentsch et al., 1982). However, after habituation, they become hypoactive (Gentsch et al., 1981) or less percent preference to that environment (Hall et al., 1997). Note this "bipolar" trait appears useful in interpreting some cognitive profile of IR, which would be discussed later.

Stress and Anxiety

Generally, IR rats have an enhanced behavioral response in situations which evoke "fear" and "anxiety" in rats, such as handling, acute restraint stress, footshock, forced swimming, tail pinch and elevated X-maze (Plaznik et al., 1993; Heritch et al., 1990; Sahakian and Robbins, 1977, Wright et al., 1991b), and some of these anxious behaviors can be reversed by benzodiazepines (Einon and Tye, 1975).

Cognitive Function

IR rats manifest a degree of "inflexible" or "perseverative" nature in changing contingencies. For example, they have shown deficits in task performance on a response transfer (Morgan, 1973), alteration (Morgan et al., 1975) and reversal (Jones et al., 1991). IR rats may also have deficits in "filtering out" stimuli, as in prepulse inhibition (PPI) of acoustic startle response (Geyer et al., 1993) in which a week leading stimulus (prepulse) markedly reduces the response to strong startle-eliciting stimulus (Ison and Hoffman, 1983; Braff et al., 1992; Geyer et al., 2001).

Neurochemical Effects

IR rats have shown an up-regulation of dopamine function presynaptically in the striatum (Jones et al., 1992; Wilkinson et al., 1994), with a possible compensatory down regulation of postsynaptic D2 receptors (Hall et al., 1998). In contrast with subcortical region, IR effects in the prefrontal cortex revealed an opposite presynaptic outcome, i.e., a down-regulation (Blanc et al., 1980; Jones et al., 1992). Interestingly, the effect of IR on serotonin in the hippocampus is operated presynaptically and accompanied by a postsynaptic up-regulation (Bickerdike et al., 1993; Wright et al., 1991a).

Social Need and Social Deprivation

Rat paradigm of social deprivation extends the attachment hypothesis of Bowlby to a more realistic realm, that is, whether it is possible that individual can develop an attachment during or after the deprivation (as seen in that the social deprivation-induced effects are evaluated when the rats are grown up). This is particularly relevant in the socially isolated rats, since the attachment or bond to peers presumably would be altered by the lack of social play, and in turn it could be either "under-developed" or over-developed in a distorted way of sociality. Most of the evidence so far demonstrated a decreased social need after the isolation period (Hol et al., 1999; Van den Berg et al., 1999; Lukkes et al., 2009a).

It is unexpected, however, that the social need may become greater if it is in a competition with food. For example, Ikemoto and Panksepp demonstrated that the isolates, when tested as juveniles, exhibit increased preference for social interactions, even over food (Ikemoto and Panksepp, 1992). This perfectly parallels with what was observed in Harlow' s monkey in which the primary need, such as food, becomes less necessary than attachment (Meyer et al., 1975).

Taken together, the distorted social need of IR rats depends largely on the experimental protocol and to what extent it interacts with some other basic needs, including food. Mechanism underlying the changed social preference remains unclear, however at least it is less to do with the temperament of the re-housed animals, whether they are previously isolated or grouped reared (Vanderschuren and Trezza, 2014). Note the IR rats are lack of a peer connection starting from scratch. In other words, they do not loss what they already have, thus the altered social need could not explain unitarily by a compensatory or rebound phenomenon for the loss of social connection.

Interpretations of IR Effects

The inconsistency of IR effects as mentioned above should not be regarded just coincident. It exemplifies some multi-faceted characters of social isolation, and for each may have different interpretations. These interpretations are not mutually exclusively, yet based on where the experimental purpose goes and what the protocol and methods are employed. They may serve for approaching distinctive mechanisms, including critical period-related developmental specificity, and the persistent effects of social connection/deprivation.

If we interpret the IR effects again by looking at more details behinds the experimental protocol of these studies, some new insights come out, and which help to elaborate the developmental hypothesis. First, the arousal level is a determinant for the stimuli or reward associated performance of IR rats (Hall et al., 1997). This is of relevance because it has been argued for a long time that the discrepancy of IR effects might be due to the differences of experimental design or environmental setting, as they are highly attributive to the arousal state. Another point, follows the arousal hypothesis, is that the contextual difference is relevant to dopaminergic activity directly (Haddon JE, Killcross S, 2011) or indirectly (Badiani et al., 2000), exemplifying the high sensitivity to dopaminergic manipulations of IR rats;. I will discuss this in detail later.

Third and probably the most intriguing one, is that a lot of attempts are made to address the importance of developmental timing and length, as seen in finding locating a critical period for a given IR effects (Liu et al., 2011; Varty et al., 1999; Wilkinson et al., 1994), and demonstrating the effects of developmental persistence, the latter is less relevant to the critical period theory, but pertinent in interpreting the long-term effects across developmental stages, thus is equally important. For example, by employing a protocol of 8-week postweaning social isolation before re-socialization, Varty and colleagues (1999) reported that continuous postweaning isolation was compulsorily required to induce PPI deficit (i.e., critical period in early life is not necessary), whereas Liu and colleagues (2011) used a similar protocol but with a longer isolation duration (10 weeks), supported the existence of critical developmental window. The same group further used a more longer duration of postweaning social isolation (i.e., 11 weeks) to contrast the persistent effects of social connection/deprivation by demonstrating that the startling habituation was impaired in the continuous IR rats under a disruption of circadian rhythm (Chang et al., 2014), implicating the accumulative role of long-term social deprivation in the pathophysiology underlying schizophrenic-spectrum disorders. The research interest in a way reflects the reality of clinical utility, as it is acknowledged that the long-term or whole life social separation is rather rare in our society nowadays, as compared to the social separation occurring only at early life stage. Several implications to interpret the effects of social isolation are discussed below.

Developmental Specificity and Critical Period

For the prerequisite of IR, animals are isolated reared since weaning. It is accordingly that all stages important for neurocognitive development would be involved, therefore it is necessary to clarify to what extent the effects of IR are developmentally specific. If the developmental specificity is necessary, a critical period should be hypothetically existed. In other words, beyond that time window, the IR effects are fixed and irreversible. As a fact, this developmental specificity has been confirmed in many IR-induced phenomena [such as in hyperactivity and impaired performance of PPI (Hall, 1998)] which, in a way, reflects a fact that some early life activity is a "must have" experience, and only serve its utility at the designated period of life time. In this regard, rats reared in social isolation obviously do lack something during important for their development.

In contrast to maternal deprivation where rats experience a disruption of an already developed bond with the dam, rats in IR are raised in a situation not allowing the development of normal attachment bond among peers. Accordingly, hypothetical peer bonds fail to develop because of a lack of various forms of physical social contact, for example, allogrooming, chasing, and fighting. Deprivation of "play-fighting" in appears to be particularly detrimental. Play-fighting (also known as "social play", as it involves strong interactions among animals) is a collection of rough-and-tumble activities by which rat approaches and pounces upon its opponent, resulting in both "wrestling" in the "on-back" and "on-top" positions (Baenninger, 1967; Takahashi and Lore, 1983; Graham and Burghardt, 2010).

Taken together, the IR-related effects are multi-faceted, and are not necessarily have to be mutually connected. To a given IR effect, it is based on its own biological profile which determines whether it is subjected to critical time window in terms of developmental hypothesis (for example, IR-impaired PP) or not (for example, IR-increased locomotor activity) (see Liu et al., 2011).

It has to be mentioned that in the interpretation of developmental hypothesis, the program of postweaning social isolation can be launched at different time points before puberty. For example, rats can be isolated immediately after the weanling and keep the isolation for two (Han et al., 2011) or three weeks (Lukkes et al., 2009), or isolated as juvenile (i.e., one weeks after weaning) for only one week (Diergaarde et al., 2004). Based on critical period hypothesis, all these protocols address some merits in approaching clinical mental dysfunctions. However, problems may lie in that as the IR rats being tested for their behavioral performance during re-socialization, the social interaction with the unfamiliar partner appears a brand new issue for the IR rats to learn. This is apparently different from situations that re-socialized rats have previously experienced some kind of social connection (for example, isolation only conducted PND 30-45, see McCormick et al., 2010), in which the sociality for them is a thing of revisiting, rather than brand-new learning. The social emotionality of these two categories is thus different, which makes data interpretation difficult. On the other hand, if the research primarily addresses enduring isolation effect, social isolation conducted from weaning to adulthood without re-socialization is legitimately the one to be most employed.

PERSISTENT SOCIAL DEPRIVATION

As we mentioned, early life experience appears to have enduring effects across the life journey. The time of testing therefore crucially determines the outcome of postweaning social isolation, particularly the acquisition of most of the behavioral tests requiring age-dependent response, selection, and sequencing. For this, post-pubertal rather than pre-pubertal approach is more appropriately to be employed (Paulus et al., 1998). Thus, in a cognitive term, the long-term isolation program is more reasonable and legitimate to reflect how the individual confronts to a previous, perhaps no longer existed, adverse environment/event. This is particularly relevant to IR paradigm when combined with a re-socialization program, as the latter would expect successfully to reverse a given IR-induced abnormality if the critical period does not existed (varty et al., 1999), or unsuccessfully to reverse it if the critical period does exist (Liu et al., 2011; Wilkinson et al., 1994). However, from cradle to grave (Chopik et al., 2013), the process of development is quite a long journey and should not confine within the early life stage only. It is imperative and probably more necessary to realize how the individual adapts behaviorally, cognitively, and even neurochemically if the adverse environment/event has not removed ever. Therefore it is better to regard the change of animals performance as an outcome of adaptation, instead of reaction, as it is clear that the animal would not expect that the isolation procedure is going to finish thus they should be psychologically prepared to bear such environment/event permanently.

Form this point of view, the persistent IR rats are particularly useful to tackle what happens during such a long term adaptation, not only explicitly the behavioral deficits, but also neurochemical, immunological and even mitochondrial abnormalities (Moller et al., 2013). As never being re-socialized, IR-induced cognitive change is less confounded by social emotionality compared with the re-socialized IR rats (Ikemoto and Panksepp, 1992; Vanderschuren and Trezza, 2014), therefore earns more research interest by as analyzing animals' behaviors which are less emotion affected, for example, testing the IR effects in startle reflex, in which social interaction in early life or for the whole life~~,~~ functions differently to the sensorimotor gating (Chang et al., 2014).

BEHAVIORAL INHIBITION

Behavioral inhibition is a spectrum of cognitive characters in which individual explicitly restrains his vigorous ongoing actions [for example, go/no-go experiment (Eagle et al., 2008)] and implicitly makes a prudent decision among ~~the~~ multiple choices based on stimulus information collected from environmental context (for example, five-choice serial reaction time task, (5-CSRTT), see Chudasama and Robbins, 2004) or outcome evaluation [~~(~~for example, delayed reinforcement task (DRT), see Cardinal et al., 2004~~)~~]. Research of the influence of social isolation on behavioral inhibition earns more attention because the involvements of social isolation-relevant neurosubstrates and brain areas, including prefrontal cortex (PFC) and nucleus accumbens (NAc) are also controlling behavioral inhibition.

For rats being socially isolated after weaning, dopamine and serotonin signaling ~~is~~ are decreased and increased, respectively, in the PFC (Fone and Porkess, 2008). Baarendse and colleagues (2013) examined the effects of social isolation both 5-CSRTT and DRT by socially isolating rats from postnatal day 21 to 42 followed by re-socialization. Their results demonstrated that social isolation during the juvenile and early adolescent stages did not affect rats' impulsive choice yet increased their premature responding as test conditions became more demanding in an unexpected manner. In other words, social isolated rats are not equally impulsive with their social controls, and only the condition requiring more behavioral inhibition, isolates exhibit a poor control of impulsiveness. This is to a degree in contrast with the previous knowledge that social isolates at the baseline condition are behaviorally more impulsive and neurochemically are of a higher uptake of $[^3H]$dopamine in the medial PFC (Wood et al., 2012), the latter indicates an increase in functioning of the dopamine transporter (see Zhu et al, 2004). Interestingly, under the challenged conditions of the 5-CSRTT (i.e., increasing intertrial interval or decreasing the stimulus duration) which are usually used to prompt the impulsive action, isolated rats were less sensitive to amphetamine. The authors interpreted their findings by suggesting that the lack of juvenile social play downgrades the ability to adapt the changeable circumstance in which the dopamine functions become lethargic (i.e., amphetamine desensitization). This is quite different with previous concept that dopamine function is expected to be energetic or strengthened by amphetamine under conditioned context (amphetamine sensitization, see Lapiz et al., 2001 for review).

It is possible that the re-socialization-caused emotional change plays a role in the transition of dopamine function from energetic to lethargic. Such a bipolar characteristic is not uncommon in social isolated rats, especially when it is relevant to dopamine-associated effects as seen previously in the contest between primary need and social need (Hall et al., 1997), which in a way may consider a deviation of biological normalization. One of the explanations could be relevant to the animals' social environment of housing condition at the time of testing, that is, amphetamine sensitization develops in rats being still isolated (Ahmed et al., 1995), whereas ~~for~~ amphetamine desensitization ~~is found~~ develops in rats being re-socialized at testing (Baarendse et al., 2013).

CUMULATIVE STRESS AND MISMATCH HYPOTHESIS

If considering that the IR procedure is an adverse manipulation, as it violates the nature of rats that they should live together in a communal organization after weanling, the longer the isolation, with adding other acute or chronic stressful experiences, ~~,~~ would contribute to the overall vulnerability based on cumulative stress hypothesis (McEwen, 1998; Taylor, 2010). The add-on adversities enters into an irreversible progress (or it is closely to the diathesis-stress model, see Jones and Fernyhough, 2007), renders a greater psychosis risk (Brown, 2011; Heins et al., 2011), thus strengthen the legitimacy of employing continuous social isolation to model clinical schizophrenia.

On the other hand, the mismatch hypothesis stands on the contrary end, holding that the add-on adversve event sometimes benefits the individual. For example, an impairment of PPI in rats being exposed to 24h-MD as pups before weanling. However, if the MD rats were reared in IR procedure, the PPI remains intact (Ellenbroek and Cools, 2002). The IR procedure is undoubtedly inherited with a stress nature as the similar result can be observed when corticosterone, an acknowledged stress hormone, is administered post puberty (Choy et al., 2008a and b), yet these rats somehow overcome the stress. The unexpected result earns itself the term of mismatch, which is apparently not impartial, with certainly quite negative point of view for interpreting stress.

The mismatch hypothesis in fact raises a previous, but not inappropriate, postulation that individuals undergo a persistent stress might develop an ability to cope with the stress. As suggested by Danysz and colleagues (1998), the persistent stress itself may resemble the chronic antidepressant treatment. As aging would be an important advantage in cultivating stress coping ability (Yang et al., 2015), the longer the IR persistence, the more possibility for rats to establish this remedial capacity. It is quite possible that a long term IR, or in other words, persistent IR, helps individuals to set up an adaptive strategy for them to control the environment.

Isolation Rearing and Hyperdopaminergic Activity

The stress-adapted strategy, if existed in IR rats, is implicated with the dopaminergic activity within CNS, as demonstrated by both non-cognitive (for example, PPI is impaired in both IR rats and amphetamine sensitized rats, see Tenn et al., 2003), and cognitive functions [for example, IR strengthens dopaminergic sensitivity in a conditioned context (for review, see Lapiz et al., 2001)]. In terms of this, while most evidence has shown that the amphetamine-sensitized behaviors are emitted positively (that is, increasing the occurrence of given activities, such as stereotypy or locomotor activity), sensitization can also be induced in which the low dose of amphetamine is found to reduce the frequency of the given activity, such as in the condition of psychogenic or schedule-induced polydipsia (SIP) (Mittleman et al., 1994; Liu et al., 2009 and 2011), the latter is considered to develop to cope with frustration or anxiety via a burst of excessive vigorous drinking (Falk, 1971).

Interestingly, the above phenomenon is not just a unique occurrence, it happens in socially isolated rats as well, and is not caused by any increase of locomotor activity (Jones et al., 1989). Specifically, the paradigm of social isolation substantially impairs the development of SIP, and it is only occurs in the life-long isolation rats (the IR rats), not the rats isolated after puberty (the IH rats) (Jones et al., 1989). These effects, when taken together, suggest a shared underlying mechanism of IR and hyperdopaminergic activity, and it is more plausible that the ongoing IR, but not the re-socialized program, renders dopamine hyperactive. In fact, the dopamine sensitization may serve as a common mechanism underlying the IR effects and the clinical schizophrenia. Similar to the psychotic symptoms in schizophrenia, some of the amphetamine-disrupted brain functions are irreversible and is susceptible to relapse even after long-term recovery (Sato et al., 1983), possibly corresponding to the neuroadaptation developed in IR rats.

STRESS OR ANTI-STRESS

The above discussion raises a quite fundamental question. Does the introduction of social isolation stresses the animals indeed? The rationale that considering social isolation is a stressful paradigm is based on the evidence that the function of central norepinephrine is employed to interpret the effects of both IR (Weinstock and Speiser, 1983) and stress (Charney and Redmond, 1983). However, the turnover rate of PFC dopamine, the neurosubstrate that is important in interpreting IR effects, is moderate changed or becomes lower in IR rats (Blanc et al., 1980; Leng et al., 2004) but higher in stressed rats (Claustre et al., 1986).

In fact, the issue whether social isolation renders animal stress or anti-stress has been questioned for a long time. Holson and colleagues had ever interrogated the legitimacy of regarding social isolation as a stress syndrome and argued that the methodologies being employed may influence the outcome in a great extent (Holson et al., 1991). Taken together the information that can be collected so far, as mentioned in this review, it is possible that among factors influencing the outcomes of social isolation, at what time and for how long for the social need to be deprived are important.

The early starting of the isolation program, as done immediately after weaning, would lead to critical period–related effects which can not be reversed by re-socialization; whereas the longer the isolation program is executed, more possible the anti-stress ability is established, and also the more times the testing is executed, the more adaptive activities and strategies can be carried out given the evidence that novelty is a determinant to adjust the outcome of social isolation (Hall et al., 1997).

Clinical Implications

One of the major utility of examining the effects of postweaning social isolation paradigm is it provides some helpful insight into the understanding of certain human mental disorders, such as ADHD and schizophrenia. For ADHD, isolates exhibit a nonspecific but robust hyperactivity and specifically a higher functioning of the dopamine transporter in medial PFC (Yates et al., 2012). The long-lasting effects on the PFC circuits in fact implicates highly with the control of cognitive function, such as the regulation of impulsivity and decision-making process. As demonstrated by Baarendse and colleagues (2013), this depends largely on the social experience during the juvenile and early adolescent stage.

For schizophrenia, IR appears to alter neurochemical function in the hippocampus, an area being thought to play a crucial role in the pathophysiology of schizophrenia, based on the evidence a disorientation of hippocampal pyramidal cell in schizophrenic patients (Conrad et al., 1991). Perhaps a more solid evidence is that neonatal excitotoxic hippocampal damage leads to a post-pubertal impairment in the PPI (Lipska et al., 1995), a deficit seen in schizophrenic spectrum disorder (Geyer et al., 2001). Thus postweaning social isolation and neonatal hippocampal damage share common consequences, such as impaired PPI and sociality, and an up-regulation of mesolimbic dopamine function. Particularly, IR-induced PPI deficit is developmentally specific in terms of the existence of early life critical period (Cilia et al., 2001; Liu et al., 2011; Wilkinson et al., 1994). In contrast, IR-induced deficit in startle habituation is more liable to be observed after the persistent IR, rather than the resocialized IR paradigm (Chang et al., 2014). Clinically, the impairment of startle habituation may implicate the rigid or inflexible character of schizophrenic patients (Braff et al., 1992; Woodward et al., 2008). In this regards, the critical period hypothesis and persistent social isolation are equally important in modeling schizophrenia-spectrum disorders. It is possible that the adaptive process is more likely to be affected by an ongoing, accumulative deprivation of social need. This implication parallels the clinical observations that the PPI impairment can be detected in the prodromal or early stage of schizophrenia (Quednow et al., 2008), whereas the dysfunction of startle habituation is usually detectable when the symptoms are full-blown (Ludewig et al., 2003), in which patients may endure longer and/or accumulative neuronal impacts. In a recent study, Ko and Liu took a further step reported that IR may play a primary role in schizophrenia-related cytokine and metabolic abnormalities, which, in a way collabotates the inflammatory hypothesis of the disease and also implies that antipsychotics are not the only cause for the metabolic syndrome in schizophrenic patients (Ko and Liu, 2015).

REFERENCES

Ahmed SH, Stinus L, Le Moal M, Cador M. Social deprivation enhances the vulnerability of male Wistar rats to stressor- and amphetamine-induced behavioral sensitization. *Psychopharmacology.* 1995,117(1):116-24.

Badiani A, Oates MM, Robinson TE. Modulation of morphine sensitization in the rat by contextual stimuli. *Psychopharmacology.* 2000, 151(2-3):273-82.

Baenninger LP. Comparison of behavioural development in socially isolated and grouped rats. *Anim Behav.* 1967, 15(2):312-23.

Beilin, Harry, Jean Piaget's enduring contribution to developmental psychology. In Parke, Ross D. (Ed); Ornstein, Peter A. (Ed); Rieser, John J. (Ed); Zahn-Waxler, Carolyn (Ed), (1994). A century of developmental psychology., (pp. 257-290). Washington, DC, US: American Psychological Association, xi, 684 pp.

Bickerdike MJ, Wright IK and Marsden CA. Social isolation attenuates rat forebrain 5HT release induced by KCl stimulation and exposure to a novel environment. *Behav Pharmacology.* 1983, 4:231-236.

Blanc G, Herve D, Simon H, Lisoprawski A, Glowinski J, Tassin JP. Response to stress of mesocortico-frontal dopaminergic neurones in rats after long-term isolation. *Nature.* 1984, 284(5753):265-7.

Bowlby J. *Attachment.* Attachment and Loss (vol. 1) (2nd ed.). 1969, New York: Basic Books

Braff DL, Grillon C and Geyer MA. Gating and habituation of the startle reflex in schizophrenic patients. *Arch Gen Psychiatry.* 1992, 49:206-15.

Brown AS. The environment and susceptibility to schizophrenia. *Prog Neurobiol.* 2011,93(1):23-58.

Cardinal RN, Winstanley CA, Robbins TW, Everitt BJ. Limbic corticostriatal systems and delayed reinforcement. *Ann N Y Acad Sci.* 2004,1021:33-50.

Chang HA, Liu YP, Tung CS, Chang CC, Tzeng NS, Huang SY. Effects of REM sleep deprivation on sensorimotor gating and startle habituation in rats: role of social isolation in early development. *Neurosci Lett.* 2014 , 11;575:63-7.

Charney DS, Redmond DE Jr. Neurobiological mechanisms in human anxiety. Evidence supporting central noradrenergic hyperactivity. *Neuropharmacology.* 1983, 22(12B):1531-6.

Chopik WJ[1], Edelstein RS, Fraley RC. From the cradle to the grave: age differences in attachment from early adulthood to old age. *J Pers.* 2013, 81(2):171-83.

Choy KH, de Visser Y, Nichols NR, van den Buuse M. Combined neonatal stress and young-adult glucocorticoid stimulation in rats reduce BDNF expression in hippocampus: effects on learning and memory. *Hippocampus.* 2008,18(7):655-67.

Choy KH, van den Buuse M. Attenuated disruption of prepulse inhibition by dopaminergic stimulation after maternal deprivation and adolescent corticosterone treatment in rats. *Eur Neuropsychopharmacol.* 2008, 18(1):1-13.

Chudasama Y, Robbins TW. Psychopharmacological approaches to modulating attention in the five-choice serial reaction time task: implications for schizophrenia. *Psychopharmacology.* 2004, 174(1):86-98.

Cilia J, Reavill C, Hagan JJ, Jones DN. Long-term evaluation of isolation-rearing induced prepulse inhibition deficits in rats. *Psychopharmacology.* 2001, 156(2-3):327-37.

Claustre Y, Rivy JP, Dennis T, Scatton B. Pharmacological studies on stress-induced increase in frontal cortical dopamine metabolism in the rat. *J Pharmacol Exp Ther.* 1986, 238(2):693-700.

Conrad AJ, Abebe T, Austin R, Forsythe S, Scheibel AB. Hippocampal pyramidal cell disarray in schizophrenia as a bilateral phenomenon. *Arch Gen Psychiatry.* 1991, 48(5):413-7.

Danysz W, Kostowski W, Archer T. Some aspects of stress and depression. Prog Neuropsychopharmacol Biol Psychiatry. 1988, 12(4):405-19.

Diergaarde L, Gerrits MA, Stuy A, Spruijt BM, van Ree JM. Neonatal amygdala lesions and juvenile isolation in the rat: differential effects on locomotor and social behavior later in life. Behav Neurosci. 2004, 118(2):298-305.

Eagle DM, Bari A, Robbins TW. The neuropsychopharmacology of action inhibition: cross-species translation of the stop-signal and go/no-go tasks. Psychopharmacology. 2008, 199(3):439-56.

Einon DF and Tye NC. Chlordiazepoxide and isolation induced timidity in rats. *Psychopharmacologia.* 1975, 44(1):83-5.

Ellenbroek BA, Cools AR. Early maternal deprivation and prepulse inhibition: the role of the postdeprivation environment. *Pharmacol Biochem Behav.* 2002, 73(1):177-84.

Erikson E. Life history and the historical moment. 1975, Norton, New York

Falk JL. The nature and determinants of adjunctive behavior. *Physiol Behav.* 1971, 6;577-588

Fone KC, Porkess MV. Behavioural and neurochemical effects of post-weaning social isolation in rodents-relevance to developmental neuropsychiatric disorders. *Neurosci Biobehav Rev.* 2008, 32(6):1087-102.

Gentsch C, Lichtsteiner M, Feer H. Locomotor activity, defecation score and corticosterone levels during an openfield exposure: a comparison among individually and group-housed rats, and genetically selected rat lines. *Physiol Behav.* 1981, 27(1):183-6.

Gentsch C, Lichtsteiner M, Kraeuchi K, Feer H. Different reaction patterns in individually and socially reared rats during exposures to novel environments. *Behav Brain Res.* 1982, 4(1):45-54.

Geyer MA, Krebs-Thomson K, Braff DL, Swerdlow NR. Pharmacological studies of prepulse inhibition models of sensorimotor gating deficits in schizophrenia: a decade in review. *Psychopharmacology.* 2001, 156(2-3):117-54.

Geyer MA, Wilkinson LS, Humby T, Robbins TW. Isolation rearing of rats produces a deficit in prepulse inhibition of acoustic startle similar to that in schizophrenia. *Biol Psychiatry.* 1993, 34(6):361-72.

Graham KL, Burghardt GM. Current perspectives on the biological study of play: signs of progress. *Q Rev Biol.* 2010, 85(4):393-418.

Haddon JE, Killcross S. Rat prefrontal dopamine and cognitive control: impaired and enhanced conflict performance. *Behav Neurosci.* 2011, 125(3):344-9.

Hall FS, Humby T, Wilkinson LS, Robbins TW. The effects of isolation-rearing on preference by rats for a novel environment. *Physiol Behav.* 1997, 62(2):299-303.

Hall FS. Social deprivation of neonatal, adolescent, and adult rats has distinct neurochemical and behavioral consequences. *Crit Rev Neurobiol.* 1998, 12(1-2):129-62.

Harris TO and Brown GW. Social causes of depression. *Curr. Opin. Psychiat.* 1996, 9:3-10.

Heins M, Simons C, Lataster T, Pfeifer S, Versmissen D, Lardinois M, Marcelis M, Delespaul P, Krabbendam L, van Os J, Myin-Germeys I.

Childhood trauma and psychosis: a case-control and case-sibling comparison across different levels of genetic liability, psychopathology, and type of trauma. *Am J Psychiatry.* 2011, 168(12):1286-94.

Heritch AJ, Henderson K, Westfall TC. Effects of social isolation on brain catecholamines and forced swimming in rats: prevention by antidepressant treatment. *J Psychiatr Res.* 1990, 24(3):251-8.

Hol T, Van den Berg CL, Van Ree JM, Spruijt BM. Isolation during the play period in infancy decreases adult social interactions in rats. *Behav Brain Res.* 1999, 100(1-2):91-7.

Holson RR, Scallet AC, Ali SF, Turner BB. "Isolation stress" revisited: isolation-rearing effects depend on animal care methods. *Physiol Behav.* 1991, 49(6):1107-18.

Hunziker MHL, Lisa Saldana R and Neuringer A. Behavioral variability in SHR and WKY rats as function of rearing environment and reinforcement contingency. *Journal of the experimental analysis of behavior.* 1996, 65:129-44.

Ikemoto S and Panksepp J. The effects of early social isolation on the motivation for social play in juvenile rats. *Dev Psychobiol.* 1992, 25(4):261-74.

Inhelder B, Piaget J. The growth of logical thinking from childhood to adolescence. *First published by Routledge, Abingdon*, 1958.

Ison JR and Hoffman HS. Reflex modifications in the domain of startle: II. The anomalous history of a robust and ubiquitous phenomenon. *Psychol Bull.* 1983, 94:3-17.

Jones GH, Hernandez TD, Kendall DA, Marsden CA, Robbins TW. Dopaminergic and serotonergic function following isolation rearing in rats: study of behavioural responses and postmortem and in vivo neurochemistry. *Pharmacol Biochem Behav.* 1992, 43(1):17-35.

Jones GH, Marsden CA, Robbins TW. Behavioural rigidity and rule-learning deficits following isolation-rearing in the rat: neurochemical correlates. *Behav Brain Res.* 1991, 43(1):35-50.

Jones GH, Robbins TW, Marsden CA. Isolation-rearing retards the acquisition of schedule-induced polydipsia in rats. *Physiol Behav.* 1989, 45(1):71-7.

Jones SR, Fernyhough C. A new look at the neural diathesis--stress model of schizophrenia: the primacy of social-evaluative and uncontrollable situations. *Schizophr Bull.* 2007, 33(5):1171-7.

Ko CY, Liu YP. Isolation rearing impaired sensorimotor gating but increased pro-inflammatory cytokines and disrupted metabolic parameters in both sexes of rats. Psychoneuroendocrinology (accepted on February 10, 2015).

Kraemer GW. A psychobiological theory of attachment. *Behav Brain Sci.* 1992, 15(3):493-511.

Lapiz MD, Fulford A, Muchimapura S, Mason R, Parker T, Marsden CA. Influence of postweaning social isolation in the rat on brain development, conditioned behaviour and neurotransmission. *Ross Fiziol Zh Im I M Sechenova.* 2001, 87(6):730-51.

Leng A, Feldon J, Ferger B. Long-term social isolation and medial prefrontal cortex: dopaminergic and cholinergic neurotransmission. *Pharmacol Biochem Behav.* 2004, 77(2):371-9.

Lipska BK, Swerdlow NR, Geyer MA, Jaskiw GE, Braff DL, Weinberger DR. Neonatal excitotoxic hippocampal damage in rats causes post-pubertal changes in prepulse inhibition of startle and its disruption by apomorphine. *Psychopharmacology.* 1995, 122(1):35-43.

Liu YP, Kao YC, Tung CS. Critical period exists in the effects of isolation rearing on sensorimotor gating function but not locomotor activity in rat. *Prog Neuropsychopharmacol Biol Psychiatry.* 2011, 35(4):1068-73.

Liu YP, Lin PJ, Tseng CJ, Wan FJ, Tung CS. Role of dopaminergic DAD1 and DAD2 receptors in the sensitization of amphetamine-suppressed schedule-induced polydipsia in rats. *Chin J Physiol.* 2009, 52(5):280-8.

Liu YP, Tung CS, Lin PJ, Wan FJ. Role of nitric oxide in amphetamine-induced sensitization of schedule-induced polydipsic rats. *Psychopharmacology* 2011, 218:599-608.

Ludewig K, Geyer MA, Vollenweider FX. Deficits in prepulse inhibition and habituation in never-medicated, first-episode schizophrenia. *Biol Psychiatry.* 2003, 54(2):121-8.

Lukkes JL, Mokin MV, Scholl JL, Forster GL. Adult rats exposed to early-life social isolation exhibit increased anxiety and conditioned fear behavior, and altered hormonal stress responses. *Horm Behav.* 2009, 55(1):248-56.

McCormick CM, Nixon F, Thomas C, Lowie B, Dyck J. Hippocampal cell proliferation and spatial memory performance after social instability stress in adolescence in female rats. *Behav Brain Res.* 2010, 208(1):23-9.

McEwen BS. Protective and damaging effects of stress mediators. *N Engl J Med.* 1998, 338(3):171-9.

Meyer JS, Novak MA, Bowman RE, Harlow HF. Behavioral and hormonal effects of attachment object separation in surrogate-peer-reared and mother-reared infant rhesus monkeys. *Dev Psychobiol. 1975*, 8(5):425-35.

Mittleman G, Rosner AL, Schaub CL. Polydipsia and dopamine: behavioral effects of dopamine D1 and D2 receptor agonists and antagonists. *J Pharmacol Exp Ther.* 1994, 271(2):638-50.

Möller M, Du Preez JL, Viljoen FP, Berk M, Emsley R, Harvey BH. Social isolation rearing induces mitochondrial, immunological, neurochemical and behavioural deficits in rats, and is reversed by clozapine or N-acetyl cysteine. *Brain Behav Immun.* 2013, 30:156-67.

Morgan M and Einon D. Incentive motivation and behavioral inhibition in socially-isolated rats. *Physiology & Behavior.* 1975, 15: 405-9.

Morgan MJ, Einon DF and Nicholas D. The effects of isolation rearing on behavioural inhibition in the rat. *Quarterly Journal of Experimental Psychology.* 1975, 27: 615-634.

Morgan MJ. Effects of post-weaning environment on learning in the rat. *Anim Behav.* 1973, 21:429-442.

Paulus MP, Bakshi VP, Geyer MA. Isolation rearing affects sequential organization of motor behavior in post-pubertal but not pre-pubertal Lister and Sprague-Dawley rats. *Behav Brain Res.* 1998, 94(2):271-80.

Paykel ES and Cooper Z. Life events and social stress. In: Paykel, E.S. (Ed) Handbook of Affective Disorders. 2nd Edition. *Churchill Livingstone. Edinburgh.* 1992.

Paykel ES and Hollyman JA. Life events and depression – a psychiatric view. *TINS.* 1984, 12:478-481.

Plaznik A, Palejko W, Stefanski R, Kostowski W. Open field behavior of rats reared in different social conditions: the effects of stress and imipramine. *Pol J Pharmacol.* 1993, 45(3):243-52.

Quednow BB, Frommann I, Berning J, Kühn KU, Maier W, Wagner M. Impaired sensorimotor gating of the acoustic startle response in the prodrome of schizophrenia. *Biol Psychiatry.* 2008, 64(9):766-73.

Sahakian BJ and Robbins TW. Isolation-rearing enhances tail pinch-induced oral behavior in rats. *Physiol Behav.* 1977, 18(1):53-8.

Sato M, Chen CC, Akiyama K, Otsuki S. Acute exacerbation of paranoid psychotic state after long-term abstinence in patients with previous methamphetamine psychosis. *Biol Psychiatry.* 1983, 18(4):429-40.

Lukkes J, Vuong S, Scholl J, Oliver, Forster G. Corticotropin-releasing factor receptor antagonism within the dorsal raphe nucleus reduces social anxiety-like behavior after early-life social isolation. *J Neurosci.* 2009, 29(32):9955-60.

Takahashi LK and Lore RK. Play fighting and the development of agonistic behavior in male and female rats. *Aggressive Behavior.* 1983, 9: 217-27.

Taylor SE. Mechanisms linking early life stress to adult health outcomes. *Proc Natl Acad Sci U S A.* 2010, 107(19):8507-12.

Tenn CC, Fletcher PJ, Kapur S. Amphetamine-sensitized animals show a sensorimotor gating and neurochemical abnormality similar to that of schizophrenia. *Schizophr Res.* 2003, 64(2-3):103-14.

Vaillant GE, Mukamal K. Successful aging. *Am J Psychiatry.* 2001, 158(6):839-47.

van den Berg CL, Hol T, Van Ree JM, Spruijt BM, Everts H, Koolhaas JM. Play is indispensable for an adequate development of coping with social challenges in the rat. *Dev Psychobiol.* 1999, 34(2):129-38.

Vanderschuren LJ[1], Trezza V. What the laboratory rat has taught us about social play behavior: role in behavioral development and neural mechanisms. *Curr Top Behav Neurosci.* 2014, 16:189-212.

Varty GB, Braff DL, Geyer MA. Is there a critical developmental 'window' for isolation rearing-induced changes in prepulse inhibition of the acoustic startle response? *Behav Brain Res.* 1999, 100(1-2):177-83.

Weinstock M, Speiser Z. The effect of dl-propranolol, d-propranolol and practolol on the hyperactivity induced in rats by prolonged isolation. *Psychopharmacologia.* 1973, 30(3):241-50.

Wilkinson LS, Killcross S, Humby T, Hall FS, Geyer MA, Robbins TW. Social isolation in the rat produces developmentally specific deficits in prepulse inhibition of the acoustic startle response without disrupting latent inhibition. *Neuropsychopharmacology.* 1994, 10(1):61-72.

Wood DA, Siegel AK, Rebec GV. Environmental enrichment reduces impulsivity during appetitive conditioning. *Physiol Behav.* 2006, 88(1-2):132-7.

Woodward TS, Moritz S, Menon M, Klinge R. Belief inflexibility in schizophrenia. *Cogn Neuropsychiatry.* 2008, 13(3):267-77.

Wright IK, Ismail H, Upton N, Marsden CA. Effect of isolation rearing on 5-HT agonist-induced responses in the rat. *Psychopharmacology.* 1991a, 105(2):259-63.

Wright, IK, Upton, N. and Marsden, CA. (1991b). Resocialisation of isolation-reared rats does not alter their axiogenic profile on the elevated x-maze model of anxiety. *Physiol Behav.* 1991b, 50:1129-1132.

Yang SN, Wang YH, Ko CY, Liu YP (2015) Effects of escitalopram on a rat model of persistent stress-altered hedonic activity: towards a different understanding of stress and depression. 2015, *Chinese Journal of Physiology,* in revision

Yates JR, Darna M, Gipson CD, Dwoskin LP, Bardo MT. Isolation rearing as a preclinical model of attention/deficit-hyperactivity disorder. *Behav Brain Res.* 2012, 234(2):292-8.

Zhu J, Green T, Bardo MT, Dwoskin LP. Environmental enrichment enhances sensitization to GBR 12935-induced activity and decreases dopamine transporter function in the medial prefrontal cortex. *Behav Brain Res.* 2004, 148(1-2):107-17.

INDEX

D

E

L

M

N

O

P

Q

R

S

T

U

V

W

Y